Get Smart!

Get
SMART!

How to Think and Act
Like the Most Successful and
Highest-Paid People in Every Field

Brian Tracy

JEREMY P. TARCHER / PENGUIN

An imprint of Penguin Random House

NEW YORK

JEREMY P. TARCHER/PENGUIN
An imprint of Penguin Random House LLC
375 Hudson Street
New York, New York 10014

Most Tarcher/Penguin books are available at special quantity discounts for bulk
purchase for sales promotions, premiums, fund-raising, and educational needs.
Special books or book excerpts also can be created to fit specific needs.
For details, write: SpecialMarkets@penguinrandomhouse.com.

CIP data available
ISBN 978-0-399-18378-2

Printed in the United States of America
1   3   5   7   9   10   8   6   4   2

Book design by Katy Riegel

The author has made best efforts to determine the sources of all quotes contained herein.

Contents

Introduction—Unleash
the Imprisoned Splendor

Truth is within ourselves; it takes no rise
From outward things, whate'er you may believe.
There is an inmost centre in us all,
Where truth abides in fulness;
...
And to know,
Rather consists in opening out a way
Whence the imprisoned splendor may escape,
Than in effecting entry for a light
Supposed to be without.

—ROBERT BROWNING

WILLIAM JAMES OF HARVARD WROTE, "The greatest revolution of my generation is the discovery that people, by changing their inner attitudes of mind, can change the outer aspects of their lives."

You and your mind are extraordinary. You have 100 billion brain cells, each connected by ganglia and neurons to as many as twenty thousand other cells. The total number of thoughts that you can think is therefore equal to one hundred billion to the twenty thousandth power.

According to the brain expert Tony Buzan, this means that the number of ideas you can generate is equal to the number one followed by eight pages of zeros, more potential ideas than the number of all the molecules in the known universe.

The question is, "How are you using this powerful mental supercomputer?"

You have the mental ability right now to set any goal and achieve everything you could ever want or hope for in life. By using your brain—your ability to think, plan, and create—with greater precision and accuracy, you can solve any problem, overcome every obstacle, and achieve any goal you can set for yourself.

Your mental supercomputer is so powerful that you could not use your full potential if you had a hundred lifetimes.

10 Percent of Potential

When I was twenty-one, I was impressed when I heard that the average person uses only 10 percent of his or her mental ability. I later learned that the true number is closer to 2 percent. Most people have enormous reserves of mental capacity that they fail to use, that they are apparently saving up for some good reason.

Imagine that you had inherited a bank account containing $1 million and growing regularly with interest. But you only ever accessed twenty thousand dollars of this amount because you lacked the necessary code to acquire the rest of your money. The remainder of this wealth was yours, but you couldn't get at it, because you did not know the correct account number that would release these funds to you.

This is the situation of most people. They have enormous stores of mental ability that they habitually fail to use.

In the pages ahead, you will learn a series of simple, practical, proven ways to tap into more and more of your natural thinking talents and abilities. You do not need to become more than you are or someone different. You only need to become all that you are already and to unleash more of your existing mental powers.

Learn the Combinations

Life is like a combination lock, only with more numbers. All combination locks work in the same way. You turn to the first number, back past that number to the second number, and forward to the third number. If you have the right numbers, the lock opens, whether it is a bicycle lock or a great vault in a major bank.

Imagine that you knew all the numbers but one to unlock the success code in whatever you wanted to do. Lacking one key number, you could spin the dial forever and never get into the riches contained inside your mental vault.

But with one extra number, in the correct order, the vault would open, and you could achieve extraordinary things with your life.

This book contains some of the best combinations ever discovered in terms of thinking tools that enable you to make quantum leaps in your life. In many cases, what holds you back is simply a matter of perspective, your particular way of looking at things.

Your Explanatory Style

Dr. Martin Seligman of the University of Pennsylvania calls the way you explain or interpret things to yourself your "explanatory style."

This can be as simple as the difference between optimism and pessimism, the glass seen as half-full or as half-empty. The optimist looks for the good and what can be gained from every situation, while the pessimist looks for the problem or downside in each situation.

But as Josh Billings, the western humorist, once said, "It ain't what a man knows what hurts him; it's what he knows that ain't true."

Ignorance is not bliss. The failure to use the appropriate thinking tools and styles in a particular area or situation can be disastrous—and often leads to overwhelming failure.

Look for the Good

Very often, when you change your perspective, you see things differently, make different decisions, and get different results. Napoleon Hill says in his success classic *Think and Grow Rich* that "within every problem or difficulty there lies the seed of an equal or greater benefit or advantage."

After interviewing more than five hundred of the wealthiest self-made multimillionaires in America, he found they all had certain qualities in common. One of these common denominators was that the wealthy people in his research had developed the habit of always seeking the valuable lesson in every setback or difficulty. And they always found it.

Most of their fortunes had come about as the result of applying the lessons they had learned through failure and hardship to developing breakthrough products and services that eventually made them rich. But without the temporary failures and the lessons they contained, they would still be working for wages.

Here is a simple way to transform your thinking to that of the most positive and successful people in our society. Think about the biggest problem that you have in your life today. Now imagine that this problem has been sent to you as a gift, to teach you something. Ask yourself, "What is the lesson or lessons that I can learn from this situation that can help me to be happier and more successful in the future?"

Perhaps your biggest problem today is not a problem at all. Perhaps it is an opportunity. As Henry Ford said, "Failure is merely an opportunity to more intelligently begin again."

A Difference of Perspective

You have heard the story of the six wise men, all blind, attempting to describe an elephant to one another. Each of the wise men touches and describes the elephant differently. All are correct from their individual perspectives.

One touches the ear and says that the elephant is like a thick blanket. Another touches the tusk and describes the elephant as sharp and pointed. One feels the leg and describes it as being like a tree trunk. One touches the side of the elephant and describes it as a wall. One grabs the tail and describes it as a rope. The last wise man touches the head and describes it as a rock. Each of them is right from his own perspective, but all of them are wrong in many ways because of their failure to see the elephant, the situation, in its totality.

What is your perspective, your attitude about yourself

and your world? Anaïs Nin wrote, "We do not see the world as it is, but as we are."

The Great Discovery

Perhaps the greatest discovery in human history is that "you become what you think about—most of the time." Your beliefs, either positive or negative, helpful or hurtful, largely determine everything you do and how you do it.

What do you think about most of the time? And how do you think about it?

As Wayne Dyer wrote, "You don't believe what you see; you see what you already believe."

Jim Rohn said, "Everything you have in your life, you have attracted to yourself by the person you are. You can change your life because you can change your thinking; you can change the person you are."

My bestselling book is titled *Change Your Thinking, Change Your Life*. And its title's message is true.

As you learn and apply these different ways of thinking, you will begin to change the person you are inside.

By the Law of Correspondence, which says, "As within, so without," your outer life will begin to correspond to and mirror or reflect your inner life. As your inner life changes, your outer life changes to reflect this new thinking. Shakespeare wrote, "There is nothing either good or bad, but thinking makes it so."

Let's begin to learn about and think the ways that the most successful and happy people think so that you can get the results and enjoy the rewards that the most successful people enjoy.

Get Smart!

1

—

Long-Time Perspective Versus Short-Time Perspective

Men are anxious to improve their circumstances, but are unwilling to improve themselves; they therefore remain bound. The man who does not shrink from self-crucifixion can never fail to accomplish the object upon which his heart is set. This is as true of earthly as of heavenly things. Even the man whose sole object is to acquire wealth must be prepared to make great personal sacrifices before he can accomplish his object; and how much more so he who would realize a strong and well-poised life.

—JAMES ALLEN

THE BETTER YOU THINK, the better results you will get and the more successful you will be in every area. The most important measure, the only measure of the quality of your thinking, is the results you get, the consequences of what you decide to do as a result of the decisions you make.

Milton Friedman, the economist, once wrote, "The best measure of quality thinking is your ability to accurately predict the consequences of your ideas and subsequent actions." His point was that economic theory divorced from what actually happened when that theory was applied was clearly incorrect.

Consequences are everything! The only question is, "Did your idea work or not?"

Some people are confused about the importance of long-term consequences. They think that their intentions are most important, not the results. This is a major cause of confusion in our society today.

They say, "If I intend for good things to happen as the result of my ideas, my decisions, and my actions and they don't, you can't blame me."

Your ability to accurately foresee and predict the consequences of your decisions and actions is the true measure of your intelligence.

What Is Intelligence?

Intelligence is not a matter of IQ, grades in school, or years of study. Intelligence is instead a "way of acting." This means that if you act intelligently, you are smart. If you act stupidly, you are stupid, irrespective of grades or measures on IQ tests.

What, then, by definition, is an intelligent act? The answer is simple. An intelligent act is something you do that moves you closer to something you really want. A stupid act is something you do that does not move you closer to something you want or, even worse, moves you away from it.

You personally define a smart or stupid act when you decide what you want and what you don't want. As Winston Churchill said, "I long ago stopped listening to what people said. Instead, I look at what they do. Behavior is the only truth."

Action Is Everything

How can you tell what a person really wants, thinks, feels, believes, and is committed to? Simple. You just look at his or her actions. It is not what people say, wish, hope, or intend that counts. It is only what they do, and especially what they do when faced with temptation or put under pressure.

Someone says, "I want to be successful in my career and in life." He actually believes it. But then you observe his behavior. This person arrives at work at the last possible minute, leaves at the first possible minute, and hurries home so that he doesn't miss the latest episode of his favorite television show. Clearly, based on his behavior, his goal is not to be successful in his career but rather to watch television. How do you know? Because that is exactly what he is doing, every night after work.

Did It Work?

The only real measure of your decisions and action is "Did it work?" Did your action, based on your thinking, move you toward something that you wanted or something that is important to you?

There are two laws that trip people up all the time, in personal life, in politics, and in international affairs. They are the Law of Unintended Consequences and the Law of Perverse Consequences.

The economist Henry Hazlitt, in his classic *Economics in One Lesson*, wrote that human beings are self-seeking. Therefore, every action is an attempt to improve one's conditions in some way. People always seek the fastest and easiest way to get the things they want as soon as possible, with little consideration of secondary consequences.

Hazlitt said that the desired result of any action is always an improvement in conditions of some kind. The improvement is the primary consequence aimed at. It is always positive. All action is focused on improvement of some kind.

Consider the Consequences

But it is the secondary and tertiary consequences—what happens afterward and after that—that are most important.

The Law of Unintended Consequences says that in many cases an act or a behavior brings about immediate positive results, in the short term, but the long-term consequences can be quite negative.

For example, a young man quits school to take a job to earn cash so that he can buy a car, socialize, go out with girls, and have an enjoyable life. These are all positive and immediate aims and goals that young people want to enjoy.

However, the consequences of a lack of education are often a lifetime of depressed earnings, little upward mobility, and the strong likelihood of the individual's never reaching his or her full potential.

Creating Something Worse

The Law of Perverse Consequences is what happens when the results of an apparently positive action turn out to create a situation that is far worse than if nothing had been done at all.

For example, the immediate benefit of giving money to people who need it in our society is to help them and provide for them in the short term.

The perverse consequences can be that the individual becomes addicted to "free money," drops out of the workforce, becomes dependent on handouts, and loses his pride, self-esteem, and self-respect. The individual ends up much worse off than if nothing had been done at all.

In society, the primary reason for social programs, giving money to the less fortunate, is always an attempt to help them to improve the quality of their lives. But the perverse consequences can become a lifetime of dependency and frustrated potential.

Think Ahead

In chess, with many pieces and many possible moves, your success is based on your ability to accurately anticipate or predict the moves of your opponent.

In life, your success is largely determined by your ability to "play down the chessboard" and to make those moves that lead to ultimate success or victory—however you define it.

Dr. Edward Banfield of Harvard studied upward social and economic mobility in the United States and other countries for almost fifty years. He was looking for the reasons why some individuals and families moved up from lower socioeconomic classes to higher socioeconomic classes, generation by generation, sometimes starting at laboring jobs and becoming wealthy in one lifetime. Why did this happen to a small group of people and not to others?

Today, in 2015, in the United States alone, there are

more than ten million millionaires, most of them self-made; that is, they started with nothing and passed the million-dollar mark in the course of a single working lifetime. In addition, according to *Forbes* magazine (March 2015), there are 1,826 billionaires, with 290 new billionaires in 2015 alone. Sixty-six percent of these billionaires are first generation, self-made. They started with nothing and earned it all in one lifetime.

The Common Denominator

Banfield wanted to know the common denominator of these people worldwide. He summarized his findings in a remarkable book, *The Unheavenly City*, which was widely criticized and quite controversial. It flew in the face of what many people wanted to believe, that poverty and welfare were largely inflicted on innocent victims who had no choice or control over what had happened to them.

His conclusion was simple and largely irrefutable. In diagnosing the economic success or failure of individuals, he concluded that "time perspective" was the overwhelmingly important factor.

Banfield divided society into seven classes from the lowest to the highest: lower-lower class; upper-lower class; lower-middle class; middle-middle class; upper-middle class; lower-upper class; and upper-upper class.

It turned out that at each level of socioeconomic achievement, the individuals practiced longer and longer time perspective. Regardless of where they had come from, their level of education, or their current situation, their time perspective was the only consistent difference in their conditions.

Time Perspective and Income

At the lowest socioeconomic level, lower-lower class, the time perspective was often only a few hours, or minutes, such as in the case of the hopeless alcoholic or drug addict, who thinks only about the next drink or dose.

At the highest level, those who were second- or third-generation wealthy, their time perspective was many years, decades, even generations into the future. It turns out that successful people are intensely future oriented. They think about the future most of the time. Peter Drucker said that the primary job of the leader, especially in business, is to think about the future; no one else is tasked with that responsibility. This is your responsibility as well.

The top people in every society projected years, even decades into the future when they made their day-to-day decisions. They thought carefully about what might happen before they made important or irrevocable commitments.

Here is a great discovery: The very act of thinking long

term sharpens your perspective and dramatically improves the quality of your short-term decision making.

Because "you become what you think about," the very act of long-term thinking changes the way you think and act in the present, thereby increasing the likelihood of greater success in the future.

Determine Your Future Intent

In 1994, Gary Hamel and C. K. Prahalad wrote a breakthrough book on business strategy titled *Competing for the Future*. In this book, they popularized the concept of future intent.

They wrote that the greater clarity you have regarding where you want to be in the future, the easier it is for you to make correct decisions in the present.

One of their most popular ideas was that if your goal is to be a leader in your industry, you must project forward five years and ask yourself, "What skills, abilities, and competences must we have five years from now in order to be one of the top companies?"

When you have clear future intent, future orientation, it becomes much easier for you to think with greater clarity, to make those decisions today that will enable you to achieve your long-term goals.

The critical word in long-term perspective is "sacrifice."

Successful people are willing to sacrifice, to delay immediate gratification in the present, in the short term, to enjoy greater rewards in the future—in the long term.

Without the willpower and discipline to engage in "short-term pain for long-term gain," little success is possible.

The Retirement Crisis

Today in America, and in other countries, we have what economists call a "looming retirement crisis." Ten thousand members of the baby boomer generation are reaching retirement age in the United States alone each day. According to the *New York Times*, the average savings of a married couple reaching retirement is only $104,000.

This amount has to last for fifteen to twenty years in retirement. At a withdrawal rate of 4 percent (recommended), the average retired couple can draw down $4,160 per year, $346 per month, for the rest of their lives, plus Social Security.

And $104,000 is the median size of accumulated savings. Fifty percent of retirees are above that number, and 50 percent are below. Some retirees have no money at all saved up. How could this happen in the most affluent country in all of human history?

The answer is clear—lack of time perspective. Millions of people got into the habit early of spending everything they earned and often more throughout their lives. Today, fully 70 percent of adults live from paycheck to paycheck. They have nothing left over. They complain that they have "too much month at the end of the money."

They were and are lulled into believing that their spendthrift habits would never catch up with them.

The Millionaire Next Door

Many millionaires and multimillionaires today are average middle-class earners, living in average homes in average neighborhoods. Many of them are teachers, truck drivers, and salespeople. But they saved 10–15 percent of their income throughout their working lives and are now wealthy and comfortable.

With the miracle of compounding, an investment of $100 per month from age twenty-one to age sixty-five at 7 or 8 percent, the average of the growth of the stock market for eighty years, would amount to more than $1 million in savings.

The development of long-time perspective, of projecting into the future five or ten years, or even longer, changes the way you think and act in the present.

Double Your Income

In Cameron Herold's book, *Double Double* (2011), he shows you how to double the size of your business in three years. His message is simple: He advises you to project forward three years into the future and decide to earn twice as much as you are earning today by that time. This amounts to an increase of 25 percent per year compounded.

Then work back to the present, and determine the exact steps you will have to take to achieve this goal. If you increase your income or grow your business by 2 percent per month, 26 percent per year, you will double it in three years.

If you are working and you increase your productivity, performance, and output by one-half of 1 percent per week, this will translate into 2 percent per month, 26 percent per year, and a doubling of your income in thirty-six months.

Back from the Future

The starting point of developing long-term time perspective is for you to practice "back from the future" thinking. Imagine you could wave a magic wand and make your life perfect sometime in the future. What would your perfect life look like? How would it be different from today?

Then come back to the present and ask, "What would

have to happen, starting today, for me to create my perfect life sometime in the future?"

Practice idealization. Imagine that there are no limits on what you can accomplish sometime in the future. Analyze your life in the four most important areas: (1) business and career; (2) family and relationships; (3) health and fitness; and (4) financial independence.

Project forward five years and imagine that your business, career, and income are ideal in every way. How much would you be earning? What sort of work would you be doing? Where would you be in your career? What kinds of people would you be working with?

YOUR FIVE-YEAR FANTASY

Peter Drucker said, "People often overestimate what they can accomplish in one year. But they greatly underestimate what they could accomplish in five years."

Once you are clear about what your ideal career and income would be five years in the future, look back to the present, and decide the steps you will have to take to get from where you are today to where you want to be in the future.

Then take the first step. The good news is that you can always see the first step. You don't have to see every step on the staircase to begin climbing. You just have to take the first step. And when you take the first step, the second step will appear. And when you take the second step, the third step will appear. You will always be able to see one step ahead, and that's all you need. But you must take the first step.

Confucius said, "A journey of a thousand leagues begins with the first step." The first step is always the hardest. It requires tremendous determination and willpower for you to do something more than and different from what you have ever done before. But once you take the first step, the second step is easier. And then the third step. Soon, you find yourself moving steadily forward, accomplishing more in a few months than you might have accomplished in past years.

Your Family and Relationships

Wave your magic wand again, and imagine that your family and relationships were ideal in every way. What would they look like? Whom would you be with? Whom would you no longer be with? If you were married, what kind of a home and lifestyle would you have with your family? What sorts of vacations would you take, and what kind of a life would you want to provide for your family?

Then look back from the future to where you are today and ask, "What would have to happen, starting today, for me to create my ideal life sometime in the future?"

Excellent Physical Health

Think about your health and fitness. If your health was perfect sometime in the future, how would it be different from today? What level of fitness would you enjoy? How much would you weigh? What sort of diet would you eat? What sort of exercise regimen would you be following? What kind of rest and relaxation would you practice, including vacations?

Then come back to the present and ask, "What would have to happen for me to enjoy superb health and fitness sometime in the future?"

Then take the first step. Do something. Do anything. Step out in faith. And you can always see the first step.

Financial Freedom

The fourth area of concern is your achievement of financial freedom, financial independence. Project forward into the future and ask, "How much money would I need to have to be comfortable sometime in the future?"

In my seminars with business owners, we teach the concept of "the number," which was also the name of an excellent book on the same subject. It simply asks, "What is your number?" What is the specific amount that you want to earn, save, invest, and accumulate over the course of your working lifetime? Especially, exactly how much will you need to support your lifestyle on a month-to-month and year-to-year basis?

There is a simple formula for financial independence. First, determine exactly how much it would cost for you to support your current lifestyle for one month if you had no income at all. More than 70 percent of adults are unsure and unclear about exactly how much it costs them to live on a month-to-month basis.

ANNUAL EXPENSES

Once you have determined your monthly requirements, which may take a bit of investigation into your current expenses, regular and unexpected, you multiply this number by twelve to determine how much you would have to have saved up or invested if you had no income for an entire year.

If you need $5,000 per month after taxes to support your current lifestyle, multiplied by twelve, you would need $60,000 per year to be comfortable if you had no income at all.

Finally, multiply your annual amount by twenty—the approximate number of years that you and/or your spouse are going to live after you retire. To continue with this example, if you need $60,000 per year to live comfortably, multiplied by twenty, you would need $1.2 million to retire at your current standard of living. (You can deduct any pensions that you might have coming from your monthly/annual requirement.)

TAKE THE FIRST STEP

Then take the first step. Open a retirement account, a financial freedom account. This is an account into which you deposit money and never take it out, for any reason. Seek out the services of a financial adviser. Learn to live on 85–90 percent of your income and save or invest the balance. Set this as one of the most important goals of your life, to achieve financial independence and hit your "number" at a specific time in the years ahead.

The very act of determining your number, making a plan to achieve it, taking action on your plan, and continuously saving and investing will increase the probability that you achieve that number sometime in the future by as much as ten times.

Make a Decision

Resolve today to develop long-time perspective. Become intensely future oriented. Think about the future most of the time.

Consider the consequences of your decisions and actions. What is likely to happen? And then what could happen? And then what?

Practice self-discipline, self-mastery, and self-control. Be willing to pay the price today in order to enjoy the rewards of a better future tomorrow.

And then take the first step. The dividing line between success and failure is not good intentions, hopes, wishes, and dreams. It is deciding what you want in each key area of your life and then taking the first step. And you can always see the first step.

ACTION EXERCISES

1. Resolve today to think long term, to consider the likely consequences of a decision before you act.

2. Project forward three to five years, and imagine that your life was ideal in every way. How would it be different from today?

3. Decide upon one action that you are going to take immediately to create your ideal future. And then take the first step.

2

Slow Thinking Versus Fast Thinking

The successful person has developed the habit of doing the things failures don't like to do. They don't like doing them either necessarily. But their disliking is subordinated to the strength of their purpose.

—ALBERT E. N. GRAY

YOUR MIND IS EXTRAORDINARY. You have the capacity to think more thoughts than all the molecules in the known universe. By properly focusing the powers of your mind on any goal or desire you have, you can accomplish extraordinary things and often far faster than you realize.

Your mind races continually. Your stream of consciousness is about fifteen hundred words per minute. Your mind jumps from one thought to another and then back again. It takes tremendous discipline and willpower for you to control and constrain this onrushing river of thought and to channel it in such a way as to enable you to accomplish all that is possible for you.

As it happens, you can think hundreds of thoughts in a row, but you can only think one thought at a time. Because of this, you have the ability to take control of this stream of consciousness and focus your thinking, like a sniper, on one thought, one target at a time.

The Reactive-Responsive Mode

Whatever you do repeatedly becomes a habit. The majority of people operate in a reactive-responsive mode. They have developed the habit of reacting and responding continually to what is going on around them, and within them, with very little deliberate, reasoned thought.

From the first ring of the alarm clock, they are largely reacting and responding to stimuli from their environment and to their habitual or momentary impulses and appetites. The normal thinking process is almost instantaneous: stimulus, then immediate response, with no time in between.

The superior thinking process is also triggered by stimulus, but between the stimulus and the response there is a moment or more where you think before you respond. Just like your mother told you, "Count to ten before you respond, especially when you are upset or angry."

The very act of stopping to think before you say or do anything almost always improves the quality of your ultimate response. It is an indispensable requirement for success. It is also a quality of wealthy people.

Thinking Is Hard Work

Thomas J. Watson Sr., the founder of IBM, required that there be signs on every office wall that said, "THINK." Whenever they had a problem to deal with in the early days, someone would point to the sign to remind his co-workers that the more they took time to think carefully about the subject under discussion, the more likely they were to come up with a proper solution or decision.

Thomas Edison once said, "Thinking is the hardest work of all, which is why most people avoid it at all costs."

There is a saying, "There are those who think. There are those who think they think. And then there is the vast majority who would rather die than think."

Good thinking is hard work. It must be learned and practiced over and over if you are going to truly plumb the depths of your mental powers.

Fortunately, whatever you do repeatedly soon becomes a habit. Once it becomes a habit, it functions easily and automatically. Goethe said, "Everything is hard before it is easy." This definitely applies to new habit formation.

Slow Thinking

One of the best habits you can develop is to practice thinking slowly in those areas where slow thinking is required.

As we discussed in chapter 1, the important factor is consequences. Almost all of the mistakes we make in life come from not carefully considering the consequences of our actions beforehand.

Daniel Kahneman's bestselling book, *Thinking, Fast and Slow*, is a major contribution to accurate thinking. Similar to the classic *Straight and Crooked Thinking* by R. H. Thouless and C. R. Thouless, Kahneman's book explores and explains many of the reasons why we come to false conclusions which lead to actions that fail to achieve the results we desire.

The authors show how we accept information and make decisions based on partial information, selective statistics, or confirmation bias—seeking information that agrees with what we have already decided to believe.

The common conclusion of these studies into poor or sloppy thinking is the necessity of slowing down before we make a decision that can have significant positive or negative consequences in our lives and work.

One of the simplest ways to do this is to continually ask, "How do we know this is true?" before we accept a piece of information as the basis for a decision.

Two Thinking Styles

The two thinking styles contrasted are fast thinking versus slow thinking. With fast thinking, we process information quickly, intuitively, automatically, instinctively, like making decisions while driving a car in busy traffic. We react and respond with little thought or consideration.

For most of our activities, such as conversations, meetings, navigating daily life, or grocery shopping, fast thinking is both appropriate and necessary. The consequences are not important, such as whether you order a hamburger or a fish patty for lunch. It doesn't really matter in the great scheme of things.

For many other areas of our lives, slow thinking is more necessary, and even essential, if we are to make the right long-term decisions that yield the consequences we desire.

Here was Kahneman's insight that was central to making his book a bestseller, and deservedly so. He said that the biggest mistake that most people make is that they use fast thinking in making long-term, vital decisions, where slow thinking is much more appropriate.

Consider the Consequences

For example, decisions about the courses you take at college, what career path you embark upon, the person you marry, and how you earn, save, and invest your money all require slow thinking.

The more important a decision can be to you in the long term, the more important it is that you slow down, call a time-out, and carefully consider both the facts and your options.

In starting and building a business, slow thinking is absolutely essential in certain areas. Which product or service you specialize in, which customer segment you aim at, which methods of production, sales, marketing, and distribution you select, and your cost and pricing decisions are all vital to the success or failure of the enterprise.

Analyze Your Way of Thinking

From now on, ask yourself on a regular basis, "Does this situation require fast or slow thinking?"

Buy time for yourself whenever possible. Put as long a gap as possible between the stimulus and the response, between the thought and the decision. Practice the "Seventy-Two-Hour Rule." Give yourself or buy yourself seventy-two hours, or three days, to consider a major decision before you make it.

Lord Acton wrote, "If it is not necessary to decide, it is necessary not to decide."

The longer you take to make an important decision, the better that decision will be in almost every case. Continually use the words "Let me think about it and get back to you."

If someone tries to pressure you into making a decision on an important issue, you can say, "If you insist on an answer immediately, the answer is NO. But if you let me think about it for a while, the answer might be different."

Write Down the Details

Think on paper. One of the most powerful thinking tools of all is a sheet of paper upon which you write down every detail of the problem or decision. Something amazing happens between the head and the hand when you write things down. When you write out all the details, you are forced to think slowly and meticulously, especially when you write by hand rather than typing. Often, as you write fact after fact, it becomes clearer and clearer to you what you should do. This is why Francis Bacon wrote, "Writing [maketh] an exact man."

Whenever the potential consequences of a decision are significant, buy yourself as much time as you possibly can. Your final decision will always be better than if you decided quickly.

People Decisions

Fully 95 percent of business success, by some estimates, will be determined by the quality of the people whom you attract and assign, appoint, and delegate the work to. The people you choose to work with, and the people who choose you, can make or break a business. This is why Peter Drucker wrote, "Fast people decisions are invariably wrong people decisions."

The people you choose to work with or for, to socialize with or marry, to invest through or go into business with, will determine about 85 percent of your success and happiness in your personal life.

The Secret of Hiring

The top sales manager for a large company, who was famous for having hired many of the firm's best salespeople, was once asked to disclose his secret to hiring success. He said, "Simple, I practice the 'Thirty-Day Rule.' No matter how much I like the candidate, I discipline myself to wait thirty days before I make a final decision. As I meet and talk with a candidate, a person who may look excellent in the first or second meeting often starts to reveal weaknesses and character flaws that make him or her completely inappropriate over the long term."

Most successful companies and managers practice different versions of this rule. They realize that the consequences of a bad hire can be very expensive. This principle applies to business partnerships and deals as well.

Think Strategically

Of the many management techniques that have come in and out of fashion over the years, strategic planning is always ranked as number one in enduring importance. In strategic planning, you are forced to think slowly, to carefully consider the likely consequences of an action or a decision. You are designing the long-term future of your business.

In personal strategic planning, it is the same. You design your own future. You think far into the future to determine where you want to be in the years ahead.

As Michael Kami, the strategy expert, wrote, "Those who do not plan for the future cannot have one."

Personal strategic planning forces you to think slowly, with greater precision and accuracy. It forces you to think about what you really want to be, have, do, and accomplish in the months and years ahead.

It is often a good idea for you to block out chunks of time, even a day or two, to think about your future, especially in times of change, turbulence, and disruption. Go for a long walk and let your mind relax. Discuss your future goals with your spouse. Take two or three days off where you disconnect from all electronic devices, including your computer, smart phone, telephones, text messages, and any other electronic interruptions that can disrupt the flow of your thinking.

Practice Solitude

One of the most powerful of all ways to practice slow thinking is for you to practice solitude on a regular basis. Many people have never practiced solitude even once in their entire lives. They have an insatiable need to be busy and active, filling every possible minute with stimuli of some kind. But this is not for you.

The practice of solitude is quite simple. It requires that you take a minimum of thirty to sixty minutes by yourself, in silence, with no music or distractions, and simply sit there quietly with no noise or activity. You can sit quietly in nature, in a park, where there is no noise.

Perhaps the best mental state for solitude is to "think

about water." Sitting and looking at a body of water, even a swimming pool, seems to relax your mind and unlock your subconscious and superconscious capabilities.

SOLITUDE REQUIRES DISCIPLINE

When you first practice solitude, you will find it extremely difficult. You will fidget and think of things that you could get up and do. You will almost have to hold yourself down for the first twenty to twenty-five minutes.

But at that point, something wonderful will happen. All of your tension and stress will begin to drain away, and you will feel completely relaxed. You will start to enjoy the sensation of simply sitting in the silence. And at this point, your mind will begin to flow with thoughts, ideas, insights, perspectives, solutions to problems, and other inspirations, any one of which can change your life.

Just let your mind flow, like a river. You do not need to write anything down. If it is a good idea, it will remain with you after your period of solitude. It is said that "men and women begin to become great when they begin to take time apart with themselves in the silence."

If you have never practiced thirty to sixty minutes of solitude, make an appointment with yourself for your first session. Often, I would stop my car in a park on the way home in the late afternoon and sit quietly for an hour. You may stay at the office after everyone has left. You may sit in your backyard or your upstairs bedroom where it is completely silent.

It Works Every Time

Here is my promise to you. Whenever you have a problem, a difficulty, an obstacle, a frustration, or a challenge in your life, go into the silence and sit quietly. The very first time you do this, almost without exception, the answer to your biggest problem will come to you, almost like a butterfly alighting on your shoulder.

Many of my students report to me that problems that had concerned them for weeks or months were almost instantly resolved by their first practice of a session in solitude.

When your answer comes, it will be complete in every respect. It will answer every detail of the problem or difficulty. It will be simple, clear, and completely within your capabilities to act. It will solve every detail of the problem. When you arise from your period of solitude and put the idea into action, everything will immediately resolve itself. You will be at peace.

Unleash Your Inner Powers

The regular practice of solitude requires slow thinking. It requires that you stop all of the business and activity around you and just go into the silence with yourself for a few minutes. The best news is that the more you practice solitude, the faster, better, and more comprehensive will be the answers and ideas that you get from each period.

In corporate strategic planning, where the consequences can be significant, taking the time to back off, slow down, and think through the critical issues can be the action that determines the success or failure of the business.

There is a rule in time management that says, "Every minute spent in planning saves ten minutes in execution."

Whenever you see a successful enterprise, you see a successful strategy in action. You see the result of an extended process of slow and careful thinking.

Use the GOSPA Thinking Model

To help yourself and others to slow down and think with greater precision, use the GOSPA model on a regular basis. The acronym GOSPA stands for "Goals, Objectives, Strategies, Priorities, and Actions."

Goals: The specific, measurable, time-bounded results

you want to achieve over the longer term in your business—your targets for sales, profitability, growth, share price, and quality rankings.

Objectives: The interim goals that you will have to achieve to accomplish your major goals. Imagine that your goals exist at the top of the ladder—your long-term aims—and your objectives are the rungs of the ladder that you must climb to achieve them.

Strategies: The various ways that you could accomplish each objective. For example, in business, one of your objectives will be to achieve a certain level of sales. You can use a variety of different strategies to achieve your sales objectives.

Priorities: Those activities that are more important than others in achieving your goals and objectives. Apply the 80/20 rule to everything. What are the top 20 percent of actions that you can take that can account for 80 percent of your results?

Actions: What specific, measurable, time-bounded activities must you take to implement your strategies, achieve your objectives, and accomplish your goals?

This method of thinking, and carefully considering each action you must take, dramatically improves your decision-making abilities. It forces you to use both long-term thinking and slow thinking together.

The Law of Probabilities

Many people attribute their success, or failure, to luck of some kind, good or bad. In reality, when looking back at what actually happened, success turns out not to be a matter of luck at all. Instead, it is a matter of probabilities.

The Law of Probabilities says that there is a probability that everything can happen, and by using certain mathematical models, you can calculate these probabilities with considerable accuracy. In its simplest application, the law says that if you do more of the things that successful people and organizations do, you increase the probabilities that you will do the right thing at the right time and be successful as well.

By practicing slow thinking whenever it is required, you will find yourself doing more of the right things and fewer of the wrong things on your journey to success.

Success is not an accident. Failure is not an accident, either. The more carefully you think and plan before taking action, the faster you take control over your success in the future.

ACTION EXERCISES

1. Resolve today to put a space where you think slowly between the stimulus, the problem or idea, and your response.

2. Select one important area of your business or personal life and practice the GOSPA model to help you think clearly and at your very best in planning your future.

3. Plan today to take thirty to sixty minutes for solitude, where you sit in complete silence and listen to your intuition. Do this regularly.

3

Informed Thinking Versus Uninformed Thinking

Beware of endeavouring to be a great man in a hurry. One such
attempt in ten thousand may succeed: these are fearful odds.

—BENJAMIN DISRAELI

THE TWO MOST POPULAR WORDS among experienced businesspeople are "due diligence." This requires taking the time,
however long, to get the critical information you need to
make the right decision.

The biggest mistakes we make are those where we commit time, money, and resources without having done sufficient homework.

The best decisions we make are almost invariably based
on having acquired complete knowledge of the issue before
we act. We "look before we leap."

Reasons for Business Success

In business, according to *Forbes* magazine, the number one reason for failure is that there is no demand for the product or service. Whatever it is, the customers don't want it or don't want it at the price that the company has to charge to stay in business.

In 2013, more than $8 billion was spent on market research in the United States alone. This money was aimed at finding out what customers really wanted before the product was produced and brought to market.

But even with exhaustive research, 80 percent of new products eventually fail and have to be taken off the market.

·According to McKinsey & Company, a leading business consultancy, the major reason for business success is high sales. The major reason for business failure is low sales. All else is commentary.

The primary reason for the poor decisions that lead to market failure is that the key people failed to ask the right questions or to get the necessary information before the product was produced and sold.

Get the Facts

Harold Geneen, who formed a conglomerate of more than 150 companies at ITT, said, "The most important elements in business are facts. Get the real facts, not the obvious facts or assumed facts or hoped-for facts. Get the real facts. Facts don't lie."

One of the most important words in business today is "validation." Never assume. When you get a good idea, immediately take action to validate it, to gather proof that it is really as good as you think it is.

Think on paper. Make a list of all the information you have about the product or service and all the information you will need to make the right decision.

Talk to other people. Seek advice and input from others who have been in the same situation.

Hire an expert. One person who specializes in a particular area can save you a fortune in lost time and money.

Do a Google search. Put in the key words associated with your question, problem, or idea, and see what pops up. Very often, this ground has already been thoroughly plowed by someone else.

Solicit opinions. Ask everyone in your business who might have some knowledge about this subject to share his or her candid opinions and ideas. One thought or observation can change your perspective completely.

Use the Scientific Method

Create a hypothesis—a yet-to-be-proven theory. Then seek ways to invalidate this hypothesis, to prove that your idea is wrong. This is what scientists do.

This is exactly the opposite of what most people do. They come up with an idea, and then they seek corroboration and proof that their idea is a good one. They practice "confirmation bias." They only look for confirmation of the validity of the idea, and they simultaneously reject all input or information that is inconsistent with what they have already decided to believe.

Create a negative or reverse hypothesis. This is the opposite of your initial theory. For example, you are Isaac Newton, and the idea of gravity has just occurred to you. Your initial hypothesis would be that "things fall down." You then attempt to prove the opposite—"things fall up."

If you cannot prove the reverse or negative hypothesis of your idea, you can then conclude that your hypothesis is correct.

For example, you come up with an idea for a product or service. You then attempt to prove that there is no demand for this product or service at this particular price. You approach a prospective customer and describe the product or service and then say, "Of course, this is not something that you want, need, or are willing to pay for, is it?"

If your customer agrees that he does not want what you are proposing, you have a valuable piece of information to guide your decision making. If, on the other hand, the customer counters your negative hypothesis by saying, "No, no, no. This is actually something that I would be very interested in buying and using if you were to bring it to market," then you have validated your initial theory about the potential demand for this new product or service.

Be Willing to Fail

Be prepared to try and fail, to propose and be rejected, over and over. Failure, trial, and error are absolutely essential to your ultimate success.

Be your own management consultant with any of your ideas and conclusions. Ask yourself the brutal questions that a consultant would ask you to help guide you in decision making.

"Is there a market demand for this new product or service?"

"How big is the demand, and at what price?"

"What changes would you have to make in your initial

idea to make this a product or service attractive enough that people would want to buy it in sufficient quantities?"

"Is the demand for this new product idea large enough to justify developing this product rather than something else?"

"Is the market for this product idea concentrated enough so that you can reach potential customers with current marketing and sales channels?"

"Will customers pay enough for this product or service to enable you to earn a greater profit than you would with some other product or service?"

Be tough on yourself in becoming informed. Don't let yourself off the hook or ask yourself softball questions. As Zig Ziglar said, "If you are hard on yourself, life will be very easy on you. But if you insist on being easy on yourself, life will be very hard on you."

Better to Be Right

As the psychologist Jerry Jampolsky once wrote, "Do you want to be right or do you want to be happy?"

It is amazing how many people come up with a new product or service idea and then fall in love with the idea long before they validate whether or not this is something that a sufficient number of customers are willing to buy and pay for.

Keep gathering information until the proper course of action becomes clear, as it eventually will. Check and double-check your facts. Assume nothing on faith. Ask, "How do we know that this is true?"

Finally, search for the hidden flaw, the one weak area in the decision that could prove fatal to the product or business if it occurred. J. Paul Getty, once the richest man in the world, was famous for his approach to making business decisions. He said, "We first determine that it is a good business opportunity. Then we ask, 'What is the worst possible thing that could happen to us in this business opportunity?' We then go to work to make sure that the worst possible outcome does not occur."

If you can gather all the information you need, and you can neutralize or remove the hidden flaw, you will make vastly better decisions than others.

Nothing Replaces Experience

This is where experienced thinking versus inexperienced thinking can be so valuable. Nothing replaces experience in a fast-moving, rapidly changing business or industry. Certain invaluable lessons can only be learned by trial and error, by having countless experiences and making innumerable mistakes in a particular area.

Experienced people develop what is called pattern recognition. When they are exposed to a new or existing business situation, they can identify patterns that they have seen before that led to either success or failure. They can immediately anticipate things that might happen that would render the business investment or decision invalid. They can quickly identify holes in the reasoning supporting the new idea. Because of the many patterns that they have seen in the past, they can quickly focus on the critical elements that can lead to success or failure.

BECOME A MASTER OF THE GAME

In a study of chess players, from local chess champions up to international grand masters, the researchers assumed that the difference in their levels of success was the players' ability to predict far more potential moves than their opponents could make in any given game. Then they found that chess players, at all levels, seldom think more than three or four moves ahead. Thinking any further ahead than that is not helpful to winning.

Instead, they found that at each level of expertise, the players recognized more patterns on the board than a player at a previous level, which could only come from experience.

The grand master could glance at a board and almost

instantly see as many as fifty thousand possible combinations of the pieces. He could accurately guess what move the opponent was likely to make given the existing pattern of the pieces on the board. As a result, a chess champion could play and win against ten, twenty, and even thirty opponents simultaneously. He could walk from board to board, glance quickly, recognize the pattern, make a decision, and move his piece. Then go on to the next board.

Experience Counts

It is the same in business and the professions. Because of extensive experience, which cannot be gained quickly or easily, the expert can rapidly assess a complex situation and immediately suggest a solution that was simply not obvious to a person with less experience.

The CEOs of Fortune 500 companies earn more than $10 million per year on average. This is almost solely because of their ability to react and respond quickly to complex situations, examples of which they have seen and worked with in the past, and then make quick and accurate decisions that lead to financial results, sometimes involving millions or billions of dollars.

Rule Number One

Perhaps the most common advice given by wealthy people is "Don't lose money." In business and in life, your goal, too, must be to not lose money. In warfare, it is often the general who makes the fewest mistakes who wins the battle. In life, it is often the individual who makes the fewest financial mistakes who leads his or her company or division to high levels of profitability. The more information you gather before you make a decision, the more likely it is that you will make the right decision that leads to the success you desire.

You achieve this goal by taking the time to become fully informed before you make an irrevocable decision in the first place.

THE STRATEGY OF THE RICH

Bernard Baruch, one of the richest self-made men in America, in his book *My Own Story*, wrote that the biggest financial mistakes he ever made were because he had failed to do sufficient due diligence before investing his money.

Warren Buffett, today the world's second-richest self-made multibillionaire, spends as much as 80 percent of each day reading and informing himself on details that can influence the investment decisions he makes. He never stops learning and gathering information.

Carlos Slim, who was the world's richest man a few years ago, has his home in Mexico City full of newspapers from all over Mexico and around the world. He reads continually in every source available to him to give him the information he needs to make the right business decisions.

Never Stop Gathering Information

Your goal should be to become better informed than anyone else in those areas of business and life that are most important to you. You do this by continually gathering information and comparing different ideas. You remain skeptical and proceed slowly toward your decisions.

The more information you gather and the more experience you accumulate, the better the decisions you will make and the better the results you will achieve.

ACTION EXERCISES

1. Select one area in your business or personal life where you need to make a decision involving time, money, and long-term consequences. Resolve to find out every detail of the decision before you take action. Accept nothing on faith.

2. Ask others. Seek out one or more people who might have had your same situation or problem, and request their advice.

3. Seek the fatal flaw in one area where you need to make a decision to go forward or not. Always assume that one exists.

4

Goal-Oriented Thinking Versus Reaction-Oriented Thinking

Mental toughness is many things and rather difficult to explain. Its qualities are sacrifice and self-denial. Also, most importantly, it is combined with a perfectly disciplined will that refuses to give in. It's a state of mind—you could call it "character in action."

—VINCE LOMBARDI

SEVERAL SELF-MADE MILLIONAIRES, all of whom started with nothing and worked their way up, were having dinner at the home of one of their group. The conversation went back and forth about the various reasons for success and why it was that the people around this table had achieved so much when the average person achieves so little. Finally, the most successful of the group spoke up and asked, "What is success?"

When they turned to him for his answer, he said, "Success is goals, and all else is commentary."

Turning Points

Throughout your life, you will have a series of turning points. These are moments, insights, or experiences that can take a few seconds or a few months. But after one of these turning points, your life is never the same again.

Sometimes you recognize one of these turning points when it takes place. In most cases, you only recognize that it was a turning point in retrospect. As you look back on your life, you often remember small things that happened to which you paid little attention, but the consequences of these events changed you in some way and had an influence on the person you are today.

One of the major turning points in my life, and in the lives of most successful people, was my discovery of goals. I was twenty-four years old, broke, unskilled, and working as a door-to-door salesman, selling very little, earning very little, and sleeping on the floor of a friend's one-room apartment. Then I discovered goals.

The Discovery of Goals

I found a used book in the bottom drawer of an old dresser in that one-room apartment. As I glanced through the book,

I came across the line "If you want to be successful, you have to have goals."

A few pages later, it said to take a sheet of paper and write down the goals that you would like to achieve sometime in the future. I had nothing to lose. I found a piece of paper and wrote down ten goals that I wanted to accomplish. I promptly lost the list. But thirty days later, my life had changed completely. I had accomplished almost all of the goals on that list in ways that were completely unexpected.

I discovered a sales technique that tripled my sales. As a result, my income had jumped. I moved to my own place. I was promoted to sales manager, given a team of people to train with my new technique, and granted an override on all their sales. And it all happened within thirty days of my writing down a list of things I wanted to achieve on that piece of paper.

The Key to Riches

Since then, I have read, researched, studied, taught, and created programs on goal setting and goal attainment that have been used by millions of people all over the world. Everywhere I go, people come up to me and say almost the exact same thing: "You changed my life; you made me rich."

When I ask them what it was in my teachings specifically that had such a profound impact on their lives, they always tell me that it was learning about how to set and achieve goals. It was the turning point in their lives, as it had been in mine.

It is not uncommon today for people to complain and even demonstrate in the streets about "the 1 percent versus the 99 percent" in our society in terms of income. But they've got it wrong. In reality, it should be "the 3 percent versus the 97 percent."

Only about 3 percent of people have clear, specific, written goals and plans that they work on each day. The other 97 percent have hopes, dreams, wishes, and fantasies, but not goals. And the great tragedy is that they don't know the difference.

Earn and Acquire Ten Times as Much

In my experience over several decades, and as a result of reading every study into those people with and without goals, I have found that the top 3 percent earn and acquire, over time, on average, ten times as much as the bottom 97 percent put together.

Why is this? There are many reasons. In the previous chapter, we said that a mantra of wealthy people is "Don't lose money."

In terms of success, we could say that the corollary is "Don't lose time."

The fact is that when you have clear, specific goals and clear plans to achieve those goals and you work on them every day, you save an enormous amount of time. You accomplish more in a few months or years than many people accomplish in a lifetime. By setting goals, you program your mental GPS, which then functions like a guided missile to move you directly toward the target you have aimed at, taking feedback from your target and making "course corrections" until you achieve your goal.

As Thomas Carlyle wrote, "The person without goals makes no progress on even the smoothest road. The person with clear goals makes rapid progress on even the roughest road."

You have heard the saying "If you don't know where you're going, any road will take you there."

Develop the Big Three

Perhaps the very best way for you to develop the "big three" of superior thinking—clarity, focus, and concentration—is for you to develop clear goals for every part of your life.

Fully 95 percent of success is developing clarity in the first place. You must become completely clear about who you are—your strengths, your weaknesses, your special talents and abilities—and what you want to do with your life.

Then you must focus single-mindedly on one thing at a time, without diversion or distraction.

According to both Bill Gates and Warren Buffett, the ability to focus on one thing at a time is more responsible for success in our fast-moving, turbulent times than any other mental ability.

Finally, once you have decided who you are and what you want and have decided upon your point of focus, you must develop the discipline to concentrate single-mindedly on one thing at a time and stay with it until it is 100 percent complete.

Goals enable you to develop the qualities of clarity, focus, and concentration much faster than anything else you could do or decide for your life. Goals are the best antidote to "fuzzy thinking," which is probably more responsible for frustration and failure than any other factor.

Minimize Distractions

Because of rapid change and constant electronic interruptions—e-mail, texts, telephone calls, and social media— more and more people are developing a form of attention deficit disorder that makes it almost impossible for them to think clearly or to stay "on task." They check their e-mail an average of forty-five times per day, are slaves to incoming mail, phone calls, and messages, and are continually chasing the "shiny objects" of immediate stimulus.

Those who do not have goals are doomed forever to work for those who do. In life, you can either work to achieve your own goals or work to achieve the goals of someone else. Of course, the best of all is when you help your company to achieve its goals by achieving your own goals.

The Impact of Change

Perhaps the most important factor affecting your life today is the speed of change. In all of human history, we have never experienced the rate of change that we are enduring today—except for next month and next year and for the rest of our lives.

Three main factors are accelerating the rate of change and causing us to feel out of control. Our very best plans are often invalidated, sometimes overnight, by a change in one of these three critical areas.

Information Explosion

The first factor driving change is the information and knowledge explosion. Information and new ideas are expanding, growing, increasing faster and faster. One new piece of knowledge, one new idea or insight, can upset or overturn an entire industry, causing failure and bankruptcy.

More smart people are developing more good and disruptive ideas today, in more different ways and on more different subjects, than at any other time in history.

THE EXPANSION OF TECHNOLOGY

The second factor driving change is technology—growing, expanding, and increasing at incredible speeds. Advances in technology can quickly transform entire industries. Think of companies like Nokia and BlackBerry that dominated their industries until the first iPhone was released in 2007. Within five years, both of these companies were virtually gone. BlackBerry went from controlling 49 percent of the business cell phone market to 0.4 percent in that time, and Nokia stopped selling cellular phones and sold out to Microsoft. One new technological breakthrough on the other side of the world can put you out of business as well if you do not respond to it quickly and appropriately.

AGGRESSIVE COMPETITION

The third factor, perhaps more disruptive than anything else, is competition. Your competitors are fiercer, more aggressive, and more determined than ever before—except for next week and next year. The competition is focused on using each new potential piece of information and breakthrough in technology to change and shape customer tastes, develop new products and services, and render obsolete whatever you are currently offering.

Your competition is continually scouring the world of new information and technology, seeking opportunities to serve your customers with what they want better, faster, and cheaper than you are today.

McDonald's, the world's leader in fast foods, has been caught flat-footed by companies like Chipotle Mexican Grill. The Gap and Abercrombie & Fitch have been blindsided by aggressive competitors offering more appropriate and better-quality products at comparable prices that are more in keeping with what customers want today.

The equation is SOC = IE x TE x C (the speed of change is equal to information explosion times technology expansion times competition). And the only thing we know is that the rate of change is going to be faster and faster in the months and years ahead. Charles Darwin wrote, "Survival goes not to the strongest or smartest of the species, but to the one most adaptable to change."

Goals Are Essential

This is why goals are so important. Goals enable you to control the direction of change, to assure that your life and work are self-determined rather than being dictated by outside events.

One of the great secrets of success is for you not to worry about things that you cannot do anything about—factors that you cannot change. You cannot change or slow down the rate of change. But you can adjust and adapt to change much better as long as you are clear about your ultimate goals.

Today, you can be either a master or a victim of change. You can be a creator of circumstances or you can be a creature of circumstances, overwhelmed and left behind by the onrushing and impersonal forces of change that you cannot affect.

Goals give power, purpose, and direction to your life. Goals bring out the very best that is in you, enabling you to realize your full potential.

Goal Setting Brings Out the Best

Goal setting requires long-term thinking, slow thinking, and informed thinking. A key success principle is for you to "think on paper." The very act of writing down what you want dramatically increases your probability of achieving it. Remember, you can't hit a target that you can't see. You can't hit a target unless you can clearly describe it on paper.

The quality of your thinking is greatly enhanced by the quality of the questions that you ask yourself, especially in the areas of goal setting and goal achieving. Here are some questions that you should ask and answer on a regular basis so that you can maintain high levels of clarity, focus, and concentration:

DETERMINE WHAT YOU REALLY WANT

What do you really, really, really want to do with your life?

It seems that when you ask this question, it is the third "really" that helps you to develop absolute clarity about where you want to be sometime in the future. When you ask "really" three times, you drill deeper into what you want more than anything else.

WHAT DO YOU REALLY VALUE?

What are your values? What are your basic organizing principles? What virtues and qualities are most important to you and most important in the people whom you like and admire?

Most problems in human life, most confusion, can be resolved by a return to values. Your values make up your core. They are the axle around which your life revolves. Your values determine your deepest emotions. They determine your beliefs, expectations, and attitude. "You don't see what you believe; you see what you have already decided to believe."

For one week, ask yourself this question repeatedly: "What is my most important value in life?"

Don't be satisfied with your first answer. Your first answer will always be something simple, obvious, and admirable to other people. But keep asking the question. "What is my most important value in life?" You may be surprised at the answer you eventually come up with.

YOUR THREE MOST IMPORTANT GOALS

What are your three most important goals in life right now?

Write down your answer in thirty seconds or less. When you only have thirty seconds to write down your three most important goals in life, your answers will be as accurate as if you had thirty minutes or three hours. What are they?

No Fear of Failure

Imagine that you have $20 million in the bank but you discover that you only have ten years left to live. What would you choose to do with the next ten years?

This question liberates you temporarily from the limiting concern over money and resources. Most people hold back on doing what they really want to do because they feel that they cannot afford it or that they do not have enough time, talents, or resources to achieve it.

But when you imagine that you have $20 million in the bank and you must choose to do something with the next ten years, you will often see clearly what is most important to you—your "heart's desire." What might it be for you?

Six Months to Live

Imagine that you visit your doctor for a complete examination. He then sits you down and tells you that he has good news for you and bad news. The good news is that you are going to enjoy superb physical health for the next six months. The bad news is that you are going to drop dead of an incurable illness on the 181st day.

If you only had six months left to live, how would you spend your time? What would you do? Who would you spend your time with? What would you want to complete? What kind of legacy would you want to leave?

These questions help you clarify what it is that you value and what is really important to you. You've heard it said that "No one on their deathbed ever said that they wished they had spent more time at the office."

YOUR FEELING OF IMPORTANCE

What sorts of activities give you your greatest feeling of importance, of personal value and self-esteem?

Dale Carnegie once said, "Tell me what gives a man his greatest feeling of importance and I will tell you his entire philosophy of life."

What activities or accomplishments have been most responsible for your greatest happiness in life to date? What do you do especially well? What has been most responsible for your biggest successes? What would you like to do, all day long, even if you didn't get paid for it?

ONE GREAT GOAL

What one great goal would you dare to set for yourself if you knew you could not fail?

The fear of failure is the greatest single obstacle to success and the primary cause of failure in adult life. Imagine that you have no limitations. Imagine that you have all the time and money, all the people and relationships, all the friends and contacts, and all the talent and ability that you need to accomplish any goal that you can set for yourself. What would it be?

Your ability to think clearly about who you are and what you really want is central to your living a high-performance life. Asking and answering these questions on a regular basis help you to develop clarity, focus, and concentration.

Goal-Setting Process

Napoleon Hill once wrote that the key to success is to use "proven success formulas." Find out what other successful people do over and over, and then do the same things that they do. By the Law of Cause and Effect, if you do what other successful people do (the causes), you will soon get the same results (the effects) that they do.

There is a simple but powerful process of setting and achieving goals that you can use immediately to transform and even supercharge your life. Here it is:

1. Decide exactly what you want. Most people never do this. Most people want many different things but no one thing in particular.

    A major reason for failure in adult life is that most

people think they already have goals. But what they have are not goals. They are merely wishes, hopes, and fantasies. A real goal, on the other hand, is something clear and specific.

Einstein said, "If you cannot explain your goal to a six-year-old child, you probably aren't clear about it yourself."

2. Write it down. A goal that is not in writing is merely a wish or a hope. It is said that goals are "dreams with deadlines." When you write down a goal, you take it out of the air and make it clear and tangible. You can see it, touch it, and read it. It now exists, whereas before it was merely a figment of your imagination, like cigarette smoke in a large room, with no form or substance.

Only 3 percent of adults have clear, written goals, and everyone else works for them. They earn and accomplish ten times as much as the average person over the course of their working lifetimes. People with written goals often accomplish more in one year than the average person accomplishes in five or ten years.

Here is the discovery: Each goal you write down, and each time you write it, you are actually writing and programming into your subconscious mind.

Once you have written down a goal, your subconscious mind accepts this as a command and begins working to bring this goal to you, and bring you to this goal, twenty-four hours a day, waking and sleeping. Written goals are very powerful.

3. Set a deadline. A deadline acts as a "forcing system" for your subconscious mind. It gives your subconscious and superconscious powers a target to aim at. From the time you write down your goal and set a deadline, you will be more motivated than ever to take the steps necessary to achieve it.

   A written goal with a deadline activates the Law of Attraction. You begin to attract into your life people, ideas, resources, and opportunities to help you to move faster toward your goal.

   What happens if you don't achieve your goal by the deadline? Simple—set another deadline. Many things can happen over which you have no control that can set back the accomplishment of your goal. No problem. Just set another deadline. Remember, there are no unrealistic goals, merely unrealistic deadlines.

4. Make a list. Write down everything you can think of that you could do to achieve your goal. Include the people, knowledge, and resources you will need. Keep adding to this list until it is complete.

   The very act of making a list of everything you can think of to achieve your goal increases your belief that the goal is attainable. It motivates and stimulates you. As Henry Ford said, "Any goal can be achieved if you break it down into enough small parts."

5. Organize the list into a plan. The first way you organize the list is by sequence. Create a checklist, a list of all the steps, one after the other, that you will have to take to achieve your goal. Working from a written checklist will increase the speed at which you achieve your goal by perhaps five or ten times.

The second way you organize your list is by priority. What is more important, and what is less important? Twenty percent of the items on your list will account for 80 percent of your success. What are they?

6. Take action immediately on your plan. Do something. Do anything. Take the first step. As Einstein said, "Nothing happens until something moves." Nothing happens until you move as well.

7. Do something every day to move you toward the achievement of your most important goal, whatever it is at that time. Never miss a day, seven days a week.

When you do something every day, you trigger the "momentum principle" of success. It may be hard to take the first step, to get going toward your goal, but after that it becomes easier and easier. You develop more and more momentum. You move faster toward your goal, and your goal moves faster toward you. And you can always see the first step.

Goal-Setting Exercise

Here is a simple exercise that has transformed the lives of hundreds of thousands of people around the world. It is so effective because it is so simple.

1. Take out a clean sheet of paper and write the word "Goals," plus today's date, at the top of the page. Then write down ten goals that you would like to achieve within the next twelve months.

    These may be one-week goals, one-month goals, six-month goals, or twelve-month goals. But they are all goals that you would like to achieve over the next year.

    It seems that goals you want to achieve within one year are more motivational than goals that reach five or ten years into the future, even though you will eventually set these goals as well.

    When you write down your goals, use the three *P*s. Make them present tense, personal, and positive. Your subconscious mind can only work on a goal that is properly phrased this way. Each goal starts with the word "I" followed by an action verb.

    For example, your goal could be, "I earn $XXX by December 31 of this year."

Write your goal as though you have already achieved it and you are explaining to someone else what you have already accomplished.

Instead of saying, "I am going to quit smoking," you would write, "I am a nonsmoker."

Write down the first ten goals you can think of in the present tense, and make them personal and positive.

2. Once you have your list of ten goals, ask this question: "Which one goal on this list, if I were to achieve it, would have the greatest positive impact on my life?"

There is always one goal that fits this description. Once you have selected this goal, it becomes your "major definite purpose" in life.

3. Transfer this goal to the top of a clean sheet of paper, making it personal and positive and in the present tense. For example, "I earn this specific amount of money by this date."

4. You then make a list of everything you can think of to achieve this goal. Write down at least twenty ideas.

Write down the obvious answers and then the opposite to each of those answers. Keep writing until you have twenty different actions you could take that would help you to achieve this goal.

5. Organize this list into a plan, a checklist with the things that you could do, from first to last.

6. Take action immediately on one task, the first item on your list, and complete this one task as soon as possible.

7. From then on, do something every day on this list to move you toward your major goal. Never allow an exception. Do this seven days a week.

Think About Your Goal

Remember the great truth: You become what you think about most of the time. Each morning when you get up, think about your goal. All day long, think about your goal. In the evening, review your progress on your major goal.

The more you think about your goal, the more ideas you will get to achieve it. Intense goal orientation stimulates your subconscious and superconscious minds toward goal attainment. The more you think, plan, and work on your major goal, the faster you move toward it, and the faster it moves toward you.

Begin today to become a goal-focused person. This will help to unlock your mental powers, stimulate your creativity, channel your energies, and motivate you forward more than any other single activity.

ACTION EXERCISES

1. Decide exactly what you want in one area of your life, the one goal that could have the most positive impact on your life.

2. Write it down, making it personal, positive, and in the present tense, as if it were already a reality.

3. Make a plan to achieve this one goal, and then do something every day that moves you closer to it.

5

Result-Oriented Thinking Versus Activity-Oriented Thinking

It is those who have this imperative demand for the best in their natures, and who will accept nothing short of it, that hold the banners of progress, that set the standards, the ideals, for others.
—Orison Swett Marden

ANOTHER MAJOR TURNING POINT in my life took place in my twenties when I looked around and noticed that there were lots of people my same age who seemed to be doing much better in life and work than I was. They wore nicer clothes, had better jobs, and drove newer cars, and some of them even had homes and families.

Meanwhile, I drove an old car, wore old clothes, worked at a sales job, thought about how much everything cost, and worried about money all the time. This is not a great way to live.

My turning point came when I started to ask, "Why is it that some people are more successful than others?"

This question changed my life. It set me off on a lifelong search to find the answers. In the Bible, it says, "Seek, and ye shall find, . . . [for] he that seeketh findeth." This turned out to be true for me. As I began asking this question, the answers started to come to me, like iron filings attracted to a magnet.

Make More Money

In monetary terms, the answer was simple, obvious, and clear. Highly paid people are highly productive. They use their time better than average people. They get more and better results for which people are willing to pay them. They spend more and more time doing more and more things of greater and greater value.

Here is a question: What is your most valuable financial asset? When I first heard this question, I was not clear about the answer. Then I learned that it is your "earning ability." Your ability to earn money is your most valuable financial asset.

You could lose your job, your home, your car, and all your savings and investments and be left there standing on the sidewalk with only the clothes on your back. But as long as you still had your earning ability, you could earn it all back and more. This has happened so many times for so many people that it is almost an urban legend.

Why do the CEOs of Fortune 500 companies earn an average of more than $10 million per year? It's because they have developed their earning ability to the point where they can get results that are sometimes hundreds of times greater than their salaries in terms of profitability for their companies. Companies are willing and eager to pay them almost any amount because of their proven ability to generate millions and even billions of dollars in profits. And if they lost their jobs for any reason, they would immediately be hired by another large company and paid $10 million per year or more.

Earning Ability Defined

Your earning ability is your ability to get results that people will pay you for. It is not your ability to go to work, put in your time, and "play well with the other kids." It is your ability to get the job done quickly and dependably, on time and on budget.

All success in the world of work boils down to one simple result: task completion. In the final analysis, your ability to complete your tasks consistently and dependably is what makes you a valuable and indispensable resource to your organization.

Top people develop the ability to complete bigger and

bigger tasks that have more and more value. They develop the reputation of being the "go-to person."

People say, "If you want it done quickly and well, give it to him or her."

Join the Top 20 Percent

The 80/20 rule seems to apply to the world of work. Twenty percent of people are on the fast track, continually increasing their value, moving up, and earning more money. Eighty percent of working people in all fields are timeservers. They come to work at the last possible minute and leave at the first possible minute. While they are there, they use their time poorly in comparison with the people on the fast track.

According to Robert Half International, fully 50 percent of working time is wasted. Most working time is wasted in idle chitchat with co-workers. It is wasted in nonstop electronic distractions, answering e-mail, going on and off social media, replying to texts, and answering telephone calls. The average person, including managers, checks his e-mail forty-five times a day.

People waste their time by coming in late, leaving early, and taking extended coffee and lunch breaks. They read the newspaper, take care of personal business, and generally function at a low level of performance.

The Roots of Poor Performance

Why is this? It is largely the result of habits formed early in life. The first exposure to "work" is when the child goes to school for the first time. The child is surrounded by other children of his or her same age. What do you do with children of your same age? You play!

From the age of five or six, school becomes the primary play place for the child. Over the years, the child evolves through the school system, primarily focused on social interaction and playing with the other kids, before school, during school, after school, and on weekends.

Then the young adult finishes school and goes to work for the first time. The first thing he sees when he looks around at his new job is other people his same age. What do you do with other people your same age? You play!

The Effect of Habit

As a result of habit, almost automatically, work becomes an extension of school. It becomes the primary play place in adult life. It is estimated that the average person does not really start work until about 11:00 a.m. and then begins to slow down and wrap up the day at about 3:30 p.m. In between, he spends most of his time playing with his friends. But this is not for you.

Wasting your time and playing with your friends all day long is for people who have little or no future. But you are different. You see success and accomplishment at work as your springboard to achieving your goals and accomplishing everything you want in life.

Work All the Time You Work

Here, then, is the rule: Work all the time you work. When you go to work, work. Do not play with your friends, check your e-mail every five minutes, read the newspaper, or take care of personal business. Work all the time you work. If you are really serious about getting results, start a little earlier. Work a little harder during the day. Stay a little later. Pick up the pace. Move faster. Keep focused on your most important tasks. Don't waste time.

If someone wants to talk with you, you say, "I'd love to talk to you, but right now I have to get back to work."

This shuts most people down immediately. How can they stop you from getting "back to work"? Tell them that you would be delighted to talk to them after work or on the weekend. Meanwhile, your personal mantra is "Back to work! Back to work! Back to work!"

Your goal, known only to you, is to develop the reputation for being the hardest-working person in your company. Work all the time you work.

When Are You Working?

Many people think that because they are at work, they are actually working. But you are only working when you are starting and completing important tasks. You are only working when you are getting results that your company wants and needs to generate revenues and create value. Top people spend more and more time doing things of higher value. Average people spend much or most of their time on activities of lower value or no value at all.

All teaching, books, and courses on time management come down to helping you ask and answer the question, "What is the most valuable use of my time right now?" Your ability to ask and answer this question accurately, and then to do exactly what is the most valuable use of your time, determines your success in your career as much as or more than any other single factor.

Get Started and Keep Going

You can use a series of strategies, tactics, methods, and techniques to get started and then to keep going until you complete the most important task before you. To manage your time effectively and get maximum results, you begin with clear goals to which you are committed.

Some of the most important questions that you can ask and answer on a regular basis are the following:

1. What am I trying to do?
2. How am I trying to do it?
3. How is this working for me? Am I getting the kinds of results I want?
4. What are my assumptions?
5. What if my assumptions in this area are wrong?
6. Could there be a better way to achieve the results that I want?
7. If I was starting this work over again, what would I do differently?

Once you are clear about your most important goal or objective, your top priority, you can use a series of proven methods and techniques each day to get your most important task completed on time.

Time Management Tools

The most powerful time management tool is a list. You start with your major goal or goals and then make checklists of everything you will need to do to achieve that goal. In your work, you begin with a list of everything you want to accomplish that day.

Ideally, you should create your work list the night before, at the end of your workday. When you plan your day the night before, you are in reality setting a series of mini-goals for the following day. Writing it out in the evening allows your superconscious mind to work on your list of mini-goals while you sleep. You will often awake with ideas and insights that you can use to get more of your most important work done faster.

If you were not able to make out a list the night before, the first thing you do in the morning, before anything, is to plan your day on paper. Make a list of everything you intend to accomplish that day. Refuse to do anything that you have not first written down on your list, not even a telephone call.

The very act of working from a list will increase your productivity by 25–50 percent the very first day.

Don't Check Your E-mail

Discipline yourself to not check your e-mail first thing in the morning. You can double and triple your productivity by breaking the addiction to electronic interruptions, especially e-mail. Instead, resolve to check your e-mail only twice per day, at 11:00 a.m. and at 3:00 p.m. Turn off the sound on your computer that alerts you to incoming e-mails. Do not allow yourself to become a slave to someone else randomly communicating with you on issues that in most cases can wait until later, and even much later.

Set Priorities on Your List

Once you have prepared your list, your outline for the day, you set priorities on your list in three different ways before you begin working. This is another discipline or habit that can dramatically increase your productivity, performance, and output.

First, apply the 80/20 rule to your daily tasks and activities. Remember that 80 percent of your results will come from 20 percent of the items on your list. If you have ten things to do in a day, two of those items will be worth more than the other eight put together. What are they?

The ABCDE Method

Use the ABCDE method to categorize your tasks. Apply the idea of "consequences" to each activity. In time management, something that is important has serious potential consequences. Something that is unimportant has low or no consequences at all. Think before you act.

A = Must do—there are serious potential conse-
    quences for doing or not doing this task. Put an
    A next to each of the most important items on
    your list.

B = Should do—there are mild consequences for
    doing or not doing this, but it is not as important
    as your A tasks.

C = Nice to do—but there are no consequences one
    way or another if you have a coffee break, chat
    with a co-worker, or check your social media.

D = Delegate—you should delegate everything that
    you possibly can, even tasks that you like and
    enjoy, to free up your time for doing only those
    few things that you can do best and are most
    important.

E = Eliminate—deliberately stop doing all low-value/
    no-value tasks and activities.

Once you have put a letter next to each task, go through and put A-1, A-2, A-3 next to your most important A tasks. Then do the same thing with B-1, B-2, B-3, and so on.

The rule is that you never do a B task while you have an A task left undone. Begin immediately to work on your A-1 task. Once you have decided this order of priority, every-thing else on your list is a waste of time compared with your *A-1* task.

Practice the 70 percent rule. If anyone else can do this 70 percent as well as you, delegate and pass off this task to that person. Because of the comfort zone, we become accus-tomed to doing things of no or low value that we once did in the past but that are no longer important to the results we are expected to achieve.

Focus on your *A* tasks one by one until they are com-plete.

The Law of Three

One of the most powerful and productive time management tools is contained in the Law of Three. This law states that there are only three tasks that you do that account for 90 percent of the value of your contribution to your company and to yourself. Everything else you do falls in the other 10 percent.

With my clients, I ask them to make a list of every task, large and small, that they do in the course of a week or a month. Most people end up with twenty to thirty tasks. Some people come back with a list containing fifty or sixty tasks! Once you have your list of tasks, you ask the three magic questions:

1. If I could do only one thing on this list, all day long, which one activity would contribute the greatest value to my company and myself?

This answer usually jumps out at you from the page. It is usually obvious and clear. And you must know this answer, whatever it is. It is impossible for you to be highly productive unless you are crystal clear about the most valuable thing you could possibly be doing.

Make the Main Thing the Main Thing

When I conducted a personal strategic planning exercise with the president of a large company, he felt that he was quite clear about the most important thing he could be doing all day long. But as we discussed it further, it turned out that he was completely wrong. It was an important task, to be sure, but it was not his task to do. The most valuable use of his time was something completely different.

This revelation changed his career and the direction of the company. In the next twelve months, with everyone practicing this Law of Three, the company doubled in sales and profitability.

2. Now ask yourself, "If I could do only two things on this list all day long, what would be number two?"

This is not always easy to determine. Often, you will need to sit with your boss, colleagues, and co-workers and get their input. It is not unusual for you to conclude that one task is more important, but to your boss and co-workers something else you do is vastly more important.

3. Now ask yourself the third magic question, "If I could only do three things on this list, all day long, what would be the third most important task?"

Again, if you are not sure, ask the people around you. For some people, the answers are clear as soon as you ask the questions. For others, the answers are unclear. But you must know the answers to these questions. If you don't, you are in danger of wasting your time doing things of lesser value or maybe even things of no value at all.

Four Corollaries to the Law of Three

Once you have determined your "big three," practice this simple formula to double and triple your productivity and output:

1. Do fewer things. The fact is that you will never get caught up. You will never be able to do all the things that you have to do. The only way that you can get

control of your life is by stopping doing things of low value.

2. Do more important things. Work on one or more of your three most important tasks.

3. Do your most important tasks more of the time. Spend your entire day on them if you possibly can.

4. Get better at each of your most important tasks. Continuous learning and personal improvement are essential to your success, but in what areas? Answer: Get better at achieving results at those tasks that are more important than anything else.

Questions to Ask

One of the best of all time management questions is this: "What one task, if I were to do it especially well, would make the greatest positive difference in my work?"

There is always an answer to this question. What can you, and only you, do that if done well will make a real difference? Whatever your answer is to this question, you should be working on that most of the time. This will almost invariably be one of your "big three."

Review your list of activities for the day and ask this question: "If I were to be called out of town for a month and could only do one thing on this list, which one task would I want to be sure to complete?"

Whatever your answer to that question is, is probably what you should start working on first thing in the morning.

Overcoming Procrastination

Your ability to overcome procrastination and get started on your most important task is one of the most valuable disciplines that you can develop.

As it happens, everyone procrastinates. Highly productive people procrastinate just as do unproductive people. What is the difference? The answer is that highly productive people procrastinate on low-value tasks. They practice "creative procrastination." They consciously decide upon those things that they are not going to do until later.

Unproductive people procrastinate on tasks of high value—those few tasks that can make all the difference to their companies and in their careers.

Here are some proven ways to eliminate procrastination:

1. Make a list of everything you have to do each day before you begin. We have already covered this in detail.
2. Take your most important task, and make a list of all the steps you could take to complete that particular task.

3. Practice the salami slice method. Slice off one piece of a large task and do only that. Often this will get you launched into the project, and your procrastination will disappear.

4. Try the Swiss cheese technique. Select one piece of a major task, and resolve to complete that one action immediately. Often, this will break the dam of procrastination and launch you into the larger task.

5. Reward yourself. Give yourself a specific reward, such as a cup of coffee or a brief break for completing one of the subtasks on your list.

6. Work in ten-minute blocks. Instead of worrying about completing the entire task, resolve to work full blast for ten minutes to get started.

7. Have everything you need at hand when you begin. The act of preparing to work often launches you into the job itself.

8. Apply the 80/20 rule to a large task. This rule says that the first 20 percent of the task often contains 80 percent of the value of the entire job. Resolve to do the first 20 percent, and you will often break the back of procrastination on that task.

The key to success in your work is task completion. For this, perhaps the single most powerful time management technique is "single-handling."

This means that once you start work on your most important task, you discipline yourself to focus and concentrate 100 percent on that task until it is complete.

Well Begun Is Half-Done

The habit of starting and completing your most important task first thing each morning will transform your life. Task completion releases endorphins, nature's "happy drug," in your brain. These endorphins enhance your creativity, improve your personality, motivate you, and give you energy. They make you feel more powerful and productive.

When you start and complete an important task first thing in the morning, you launch yourself into "the zone." You actually function on a higher level, getting more top-quality work done faster all day long.

Focus on Results

Keep asking, "What results are expected of me?"

And of all the results that you could possibly achieve, what are the most important things you need to do quickly and well that can make the greatest difference in your career?

Whatever your answer is to this question, get started on that one task immediately, and keep going until it is complete. The development of this habit will quickly move you into the ranks of the most productive people in your business and industry.

ACTION EXERCISES

1. Think on paper. Write things down. Always work from a list or, even better, a checklist.

2. Determine your "big three," those tasks that represent 90 percent of the value of your contribution to your company and to yourself.

3. Discipline yourself to start immediately each morning on the most valuable use of your time, and then persist until that task is 100 percent complete.

6

Positive Thinking Versus Negative Thinking

> Hold yourself responsible for a higher standard than anybody
> else expects of you. Never excuse yourself. Never pity yourself.
> Be a hard master to yourself—and be lenient to everybody else.
> —HENRY WARD BEECHER

ARISTOTLE, perhaps the greatest philosopher of all time, studied the human condition more extensively than any other man in history. He concluded that the ultimate goal of human life and endeavor was happiness. He said that every act a person takes is aimed at achieving a greater state of happiness, however the individual defines it.

You want to get a good job. Why? To earn more money. Why? To be able to provide for your family and enjoy a good lifestyle. Why? To achieve personal and financial security. Why? So you can be happy.

The True Measure

The true measure of how successful you are in life is how happy you are—most of the time. If you are wealthy, famous, or powerful but you are not happy, you have failed in your primary responsibility to yourself as a human being.

Every human act is aimed at achieving a greater state of happiness, however the individual defines it. This does not mean that every act leads to happiness. Many people make a complete mess of their lives attempting to achieve happiness and often end up unhappier and more dissatisfied than they would have been if they had done nothing. They are examples of the Law of Unintended Consequences and the Law of Perverse Consequences.

The positive emotions of love, joy, peace, excitement, success, and the feeling that you are fulfilling your complete potential are what everyone aims at almost all the time.

What Successful People Do

Successful people practice positive thinking most of the time. As a result, they are happier, more genial, more popular and derive more real pleasure from life than the average person.

The opposite of positive thinking is negative thinking.

Negative thinkers tend to be hostile and suspicious. They are distrustful of others, and they expect negative things to happen to them most of the time. They have negative personalities and are highly critical of both themselves and the people around them. No matter what happens, they are seldom satisfied for any period of time. Life to them is a series of problems and difficulties over which they feel they have little control and about which there is nothing they can do.

Many years ago, when I began asking the question, "Why are some people more successful and happy than others?," I started studying the contrast and difference between positive emotions and negative emotions. What I found changed my life forever.

The Great Discovery

What I discovered is that everyone wants to be happy, however he defines it. The main obstacle between each person and the happiness that he desires is negative emotions. Negative emotions lie at the root of virtually all problems in human life. If there was some way that you could eliminate negative emotions, you could wipe out most of the problems of mankind.

There is a way to do this. Nature abhors a vacuum. If you eliminate negative emotions, your mind automatically fills with positive emotions. When you eliminate negative emotions, you become a fully functioning person. When you eliminate negative emotions, you become capable of fulfilling your full potential.

The main job of life, then, is to eliminate negative emotions.

One Thought at a Time

Your mind can only hold one thought at a time—positive or negative. But if you don't deliberately hold a positive thought or emotion, a negative thought or emotion will tend to fill your mind, at least at the beginning. Negative thoughts tend to be easy and automatic, the default setting of the brain for most people.

Thinking positively actually requires effort and determination until it becomes a habitual response to life and circumstances. Fortunately, you can become a purely positive thinker through learning and practice.

The starting point of eliminating negative emotions is to understand where they come from in the first place. The good news is that no child is born with any fears or negative emotions. All fears and negative emotions must be taught to the growing child in his or her formative years. And because negative emotions are learned, they can be unlearned.

Because negative emotions are habitual ways of responding and reacting to people and situations, they can be replaced with constructive habits of responding and reacting. This is very much a matter of choice.

Abraham Lincoln said, "Most people are just about as happy as they make up their minds to be."

The Newborn Child

Children are born with two wonderful characteristics, fearlessness and spontaneity. The newborn child is completely fearless. The growing child will touch, try, or taste anything, however dangerous. Parents have to spend the first few years of the child's life preventing the child from killing himself or herself.

The child is also born spontaneous. He or she laughs, cries, pees, poops, and expresses himself or herself without limit or constraint, twenty-four hours a day. A child has no concern about the reactions and responses of others. He or she simply does not care.

Fears of Failure and Criticism

At a young age, because of mistakes that parents make, children begin to develop the two main fears of adult life, the fear of failure and the fear of criticism. When parents, in an attempt to restrain or constrain the child's behavior, tell the child, "No! Stop that! Don't do that! Get away from there!" and, even worse, physically punish the child for fearlessly exploring his or her world, the child soon develops the belief that he or she is small and incompetent. Soon the child refrains from reaching out and trying new things. He or she starts to say "I can't, I can't, I can't" when confronted with anything new or different.

This feeling of "I can't" soon turns into the fear of failure. As adults, it becomes a preoccupation with loss or poverty. Adults fear the loss of money and time, the loss of security and approval, the loss of the love of someone important, the loss of health, and the possibility of poverty. This generalized fear of failure acts as a brake on the child's potential and then the adult's potential. It is the single greatest obstacle to success in adult life.

THE FEAR OF CRITICISM

Young children soon lose their natural spontaneity as well. As the result of parental mistakes, especially making their love and affection dependent upon the child's doing what they want him or her to do, the child very early develops fears of criticism and rejection.

When parents become angry and threaten to withhold their approval if the child does not do what they want, he begins thinking to himself, "I must do what Mommy and Daddy want, or they won't love me." Because, to children, the love and security of their parents are the paramount concerns in their existence, any threat of loss of this love terrifies them and causes them to engage in or refrain from any behavior that may lead to this loss.

LOVE WITHHELD

Psychologists generally agree that most problems in adult life stem from "love withheld" in early childhood. The most powerful and profound way to distort the adult personality is rooted in "love deprivation" or the giving and then withholding of love when the child is young.

Children need love like roses need rain. Without an endless, unbroken flow of unconditional love, the child grows up emotionally vulnerable and soon becomes susceptible to negative emotions of all kinds.

Alexander Pope wrote, "Just as the Twig is bent, the Tree's inclined." A negative childhood leads to a negative adulthood.

Deficiency and Being Needs

The psychologist Abraham Maslow, who studied the personality styles of self-actualizing people, concluded that

98 percent of adults are largely governed by what he called "deficiency needs." Instead of striving to realize their full potentials, they strove throughout their lives to compensate for their perceived deficiencies, especially those of "unde- servingness" and the feeling that "I'm not good enough."

Maslow said that only 2 percent of adults experience "be- ing needs," which he defined as the desire and confidence to grow and realize their full potentials in life. He called these the "self-actualizing" people in our society, those character- ized by high levels of self-esteem and self-confidence.

The Russian Metaphysicians

More than one hundred years ago, the Russian metaphysicians Peter Ouspensky and G. I. Gurdjieff developed a system of teaching to help identify and remove the sources and causes of negative emotions in their students. They concluded, as modern psychologists have, that if negative emotions were eliminated, all that would be left would be a fully mature, fully functioning, completely positive, self-actualizing human being. Reaching this state seems to be the goal of most peo- ple in life.

What, then, are the root causes of negative emotions in adult life? There are several. Let us explore them in turn.

The Roots of Negative Emotions

1. **Rationalization:** Negative emotions are created when we attempt to explain away a situation or a behavior in our lives that is unpleasant for us. Rationalization has been defined as "putting a favorable interpretation on an otherwise unfavorable act."

   We attempt to rationalize and explain away the negative behaviors that hold us back from enjoying the success and happiness that we truly desire in life. We rationalize dishonesty by saying, "Everybody does it." We rationalize obesity by saying, "It is determined by my genes or by my hormones." We rationalize laziness, lateness, lack of self-discipline, and poor work habits by saying, "That's just the way I am," and then by comparing ourselves favorably with people who are doing even worse than we are so we never have to improve.

   As a result of continually rationalizing away our negative behaviors, we become unhappier and more dissatisfied and fail to make progress in our lives.

2. **Justification:** Another major source of negative emotions comes about when we justify our negative behaviors by explaining them away in some fashion. We justify our negative emotions by telling ourselves, and

anyone else who will listen, that we are thoroughly entitled to experience this negative emotion because of something that someone else, somewhere, has done to us or to someone else.

Justification enables us to create elaborate reasons for problems in our lives and in the lives of others. If you could not justify a negative feeling or behavior, it would cease immediately.

3. **Judgmentalism:** Many of our negative emotions come from our tendency to judge other people. We actually set ourselves up as judge, jury, and executioner. We find the other person guilty of doing or not doing something, condemn him for his misbehavior, and pass a sentence upon him.

This is why one of the most important teachings in the Bible, and in other religious scriptures, is "Judge not, that ye be not judged." When you judge and condemn others, for any reason, finding them guilty, you immediately see them, think about them, and feel toward them in a negative way.

In the Bible, it also says, "With what judgment ye judge, ye shall be judged." This means that when you judge and condemn another person, you actually judge and condemn yourself. Even though you have found him guilty and feel negative toward him, you actually feel negative toward yourself just as much or even more. And in most cases, the other person does not even know that you have gone through this judging and condemning process. The person at whom you are angry doesn't even really care.

4. **Hypersensitivity:** As a result of the development of feelings of rejection and criticism in childhood, it is quite common for people to become hypersensitive to the thoughts, feelings, and behaviors of others as adults. We see criticisms and slights where they don't exist. We are hypersensitive to what we think other people might be thinking and feeling about us. We are so concerned with not incurring the displeasure or disapproval of others that we are often paralyzed or held back from taking actions that are in our best interests.

In sales and in business, we continually meet potential customers who cannot make a buying decision of any kind without consulting and getting the overwhelming approval of one or more people in their families or businesses. Hypersensitivity in extreme forms can actually paralyze people and make them unable to make decisions in their best interests.

The Cause of Negative Emotions

Negative emotions ultimately boil down to anger of some kind, either inwardly expressed, in that the anger makes you sick, or outwardly expressed, so that it makes others feel angry and hostile.

Most psychological and psychosomatic problems are caused by suppression of negative emotions, repression of negative emotions, depression caused by negative emotions, projection of our negative emotions onto others, displacement of negative emotions in that we become angry with others when we are really angry with ourselves, and so on.

The negative emotions most common in our society are, first of all, fear of all kinds, as we have discussed. There are also the twin emotions that drive much political activity in most societies throughout the world: envy and resentment. There is jealousy, coupled with feelings of inferiority, so that the individual thinks, "No one could ever love me." There are others such as hate, suspicion, hostility, and distrust.

The Negative Emotion Tree

Imagine a picture of the "negative emotion tree": the fruit growing on this tree are all of the negative emotions that you can experience. In order to eliminate your negative emotions, you have to cut down this tree.

Here is the great breakthrough: The trunk of the negative emotion tree is blame. It is impossible to experience a negative emotion without blaming others for something that they have done or not done of which you disapprove. The minute you stop blaming, your negative emotions cease completely.

Eliminating Blame

And how do you stop blaming? The answer is both simple and revolutionary. It is impossible for you to blame someone else for a negative emotion and accept responsibility for the situation at the same time. The very act of accepting responsibility cancels the negative emotion associated with that situation, person, problem, or difficulty.

And how do you activate this sense of responsibility? You simply say the magic words "I am responsible."

This positive, present-tense affirmation eliminates negative emotions of all kinds instantly.

Because your mind can only hold one thought at a time—positive or negative—you can cancel any negative thought at any time by simply repeating to yourself, over and over again, "I am responsible! I am responsible! I am responsible!"

How do you turn out all the Christmas lights on your tree? Simple. You jerk the electric cord out of the socket, and all the lights go out instantly.

How do you get rid of all of your negative emotions? The same way—you simply cancel them whenever they arise by immediately saying, "I am responsible!" They all stop immediately.

Accept 100 Percent Responsibility

The key to self-esteem, self-confidence, self-reliance, and self-respect is for you to accept 100 percent responsibility for everything you are and all that you will become in life. The instant you accept complete responsibility, with no excuses, you become calm, clear, and positive. The sun rises in your life, and all the shadows disappear.

There is one essential part of eliminating negative emotions, and that is the practice of forgiveness. Everyone has been wronged in life in some way by someone. We have had difficult childhoods, negative experiences growing up, bad relationships, jobs that did not work out, and investments that went bad. Everyone has been lied to, cheated on, hurt, taken advantage of, and abused in some way. Unfortunately, this is normal and natural and an inevitable part of the human experience. The only question is, "What are you going to do about it?"

Freely Forgive and Forget

The answer is that for you to be free, you must free everyone else. For you to be happy, you must forgive everyone who has ever hurt you in any way. You must openly, freely, and completely let go of all negative thoughts you still think, feel, or experience toward anyone in your life. You must issue a blanket pardon for everyone.

At this point, in my seminars and workshops, because of my reasoning, most people agree that, all things considered, they are going to forgive everyone who has ever wronged them in some way. If you agree with the concept of forgiveness, as most people do, then the next question is, "Who do I need to forgive?"

There are three types of people whom you need to forgive:

1. You must forgive your parents. You must let them go and set them free. You must forgive them for every mistake they ever made in raising you.

   Many children grow up with an unreasonable belief that their parents, being the most important people in their lives, must be perfect and all knowing in some way. The fact is that your parents are normal people just like you who made all kinds of mistakes because of ignorance and inexperience.

You must forgive your parents for every mistake that they ever made in bringing you up. You must let them go completely. Even better, you must go to them and tell them that you forgive them for everything they ever did or said that hurt you in any way. Set them free and become free yourself.

2. You must forgive every other person who has ever hurt you in any way—every personal relationship or business association, even those relationships and marriages that caused you incredible emotional turmoil and distress. You must forgive.

You must issue a total pardon to all those people you still think about from time to time in terms of negativity, anger, and the desire to punish them or get even in some way.

Remember, you are not forgiving for the sake of the other person. Forgiveness is a perfectly selfish act. You are forgiving for yourself. By letting them go free, by forgiveness, you are allowing yourself to go free at the same time.

3. Finally, you must forgive yourself. You must forgive yourself for every wicked, senseless, brainless, and stupid thing you ever did that hurt anyone, for any reason, at any time in your life.

Remember, the person you are today is not the person you were when you hurt someone else in some way. The person you are today is not the person who would ever do what you did at a previous time.

Let It All Go

You must set yourself free by forgiving yourself for every mistake that you have ever made. The truth is that in your heart you are a thoroughly good person. Any mistake that you have ever made in the past was made because of youth, inexperience, and a lack of knowledge or understanding. But it is now over and gone. Those are past events. Let them go, and get on with the rest of your life.

As Helen Keller said, "When you turn toward the sunshine, the shadows fall behind you."

Your main job in life, if you want to become a totally positive person, is to let the past go and turn toward the sunshine. Become a totally positive person. Think about the things that you want and need. Think about where you are going and what you can accomplish. Think about the extraordinary person you are and all that you can become.

The Trip Clause

I have worked with more than one million people on these ideas. Almost all of them agree that they are going to forgive, forget, and let go. However, at the same time, they plant within themselves the seeds of their own destruction.

They say something like "I hereby resolve to forgive everyone in my life who has ever hurt me for any reason. I set them free and let them go. (Except for that one person or that particular situation.)"

All psychological, emotional, and psychosomatic problems can be traced back to the failure to let go of one negative event about which you are still angry and for which you cannot forgive.

The New Mercedes-Benz

Let me give you an example. Imagine that you order a brand-new Mercedes-Benz from the factory. It is delivered, perfect in every respect, except for one. Somehow, in the process of manufacturing the car, the engineers have accidentally installed the brake on one of your front wheels incorrectly. As a result, the brake locks and the wheel fails to turn.

You get into your brand-new Mercedes-Benz and turn the ignition key. The engine starts, you shift into gear, and you step on the accelerator. What would happen? Well, if one of your front brakes was locked, your beautiful car would simply go around in circles. You could turn the steering wheel and step on the gas, but the car would still go around in a circle, getting you nowhere. The more you stepped on the gas, the faster you would burn out your engine and your rear tires.

Release Your Brakes

It is the same with your life. If you have one person in your life that you refuse to forgive, someone with whom you are still angry, it is like having a locked brake on one of your front wheels. Your life will spin around and around in circles. You will burn out emotionally and physically. You will never be truly happy, and you will never make any progress. You will think about this negative person or event over and over again, year after year, keeping your mental foot on your emotional brakes.

This single insight is the key to understanding psychology and psychosomatic illness. It is the refusal to let go of a single event, and often several events, that locks a person in place and keeps him or her trapped in the past. With this refusal to forgive, no progress is possible.

What is the one person or event that you cannot or will not let go of? Whatever it is, you must have the character and the courage to let it go. No matter how painful it was, you must say the magic words: "I forgive him or her for everything. I let him or her go. It is over."

Responsibility, Control, and Positive Emotions

There is a direct relationship between the amount of responsibility that you accept and the amount of control that you feel in your life. Because almost all stress and negative emotions come from feeling out of control in some way, as soon as you accept responsibility, you assert control over yourself and everything that happens to you.

There is a direct relationship between the acceptance of responsibility, a feeling of control, and positive mental emotions. The more you accept responsibility and feel in control of your life, the more positive you feel about yourself and your world. Finally, there is a direct relationship between positive emotions and happiness. And the choice is completely up to you.

Take Control

When you blame anyone else for anything, you give up control of your emotions. You turn control of your emotions over to the person you are blaming, whether he knows it or not. By blaming someone else for something, you enable that person to manipulate and control your emotions—at long distance. You give him power and control over your own happiness by your refusal to forgive him and to let him go.

And in most cases, he doesn't even know how much control he has over your happiness and well-being.

By complaining about and criticizing others, you set yourself up as a "victim." By blaming others, you make yourself feel small and weak, angry and inferior. Instead of seeing yourself as a totally responsible, self-reliant individual, you allow yourself to be controlled by others and not in charge of your own life and emotions. When you blame other people, you become negative, angry, suspicious, hostile, and weak. Is this what you had in mind?

Say the Magic Words

The good news is that at any time you can say the magic words "I am responsible" and put yourself immediately back into the driver's seat of your own emotional life. Whenever you experience a negative thought of any kind, immediately cancel it with the words "I am responsible!" Do this over and over again until it becomes automatic and easy. Acceptance of responsibility is the mark of a leader, an achiever, and a self-actualizing man or woman.

Resolve today to become a totally responsible, completely mature, fully functioning adult. Just say the words "I am responsible" over and over again and mean it. This is the real key to positive thinking.

✳ ACTION EXERCISES

1. Resolve today to become a completely positive person. Look for the good in every person and situation. You will always find it.

2. Decide today to eliminate the negative emotions that interfere with your happiness. Refuse to think or talk about the things that make you angry or upset.

3. Issue a blanket pardon to everyone who has ever hurt you in any way. Practice forgiveness on a go-forward basis.

7

Flexible Thinking Versus Rigid Thinking

The individual who wants to reach the top in business must appreciate the might and force of habit. He must be quick to break those habits that can break him—and hasten to adopt those practices that will become the habits that help him achieve the success he desires.

—J. PAUL GETTY

IN TIMES OF TURBULENCE and rapid change, your ability to think flexibly, to consider every aspect of a situation and then to respond effectively to change, can have an enormous impact on your business and your career.

In 1952, Albert Einstein was teaching at Princeton University. One day, he was walking back to his office with his teaching assistant, who was carrying the copies of an examination that Einstein had just given to an advanced class of physics students.

The teaching assistant, a bit hesitantly, asked Dr. Einstein, "Excuse me for asking, but isn't this the same exam that you gave to this same class of physics students last year?"

Dr. Einstein replied, "Yes, it is the same exam."

The teaching assistant then asked, even more hesitantly than before, "But how could you give the same exam to the same students, two years in a row?"

Einstein answered simply, "Because the answers have changed."

At that time, in the world of physics, new advances, theories, and discoveries were being made continually all over the world. The answers that had been correct one year were no longer correct the following year because of new ideas and breakthroughs in the field.

Your Answers Have Changed

Your situation is the same. In many areas of your life, your answers have changed. What was true and valid a year ago is either partially or totally obsolete today. Your cherished ideas from a year or two ago, or even a month ago, are no longer valid or relevant in the turbulent markets of today.

In technology, for example, they say that a product is already obsolete when it first hits the shelves. By the time it comes to the market, it is already being replaced either by the company that developed it or by its competitors. The shelf life of technology is shorter and shorter. It is the same with information and competition. The speed at which they are changing is almost breathtaking.

The Most Important Quality

In 1995, the Menninger Institute of New York conducted a study to determine the most important quality or qualities that would be necessary for business success in the twenty-first century. It finally concluded that the most important quality required for success would be "flexibility."

It would be the ability to rapidly react and respond to the accelerating rate of change in all areas. The development of this attitude of flexibility, accepting that "the answers have changed," would give an individual or an organization a tremendous advantage over more rigid and inflexible competitors.

Change Is Faster and Faster

We are living in the fastest changing, most disruptive, and most turbulent period in all of human history, except for tomorrow and next week and next year.

Right up to the middle of the twentieth century, it was

quite common for a person to come out of school, join a company, start a job, and stay there for life.

Today, as many as 40 percent of adults are what are called contingency workers—freelancers who go from job to job throughout their working lives as independent contractors. Many of them will never work for a company, except temporarily.

Two Million Jobs Disappear

Every year in America alone, on average, two million jobs disappear. The products and services that companies were offering fell out of favor with changing customer tastes, and the skills necessary to produce those products and services were no longer required. This is a major problem in the world of work today, and it is only going to accelerate in the months and years ahead.

Fortunately, on average in America, 2.2 million or more jobs are created each year. Fully 80 percent of new job creation comes from new companies offering new products and services to different customers in different markets.

Because of this rapid rate of change, many industries and most companies are operating today on the basis of business models that no longer work, or that don't work as they used to in creating a steady stream of sales and profitability.

Your Business Model

A business model is defined as the complete system, from beginning to end, by which a company produces and sells a product or service and generates profits. There are at least fifty-five different business models that a company can use. Trying to achieve results with the wrong business model for your current market can lead to declining sales and profitability or even corporate collapse.

In 2007, when Apple released the iPhone, the senior executives at BlackBerry dismissed it as a toy and assumed that it would only appeal to young people who wanted to communicate with their friends. Within five years, its market share among business owners of cell phones dropped from 49 percent to 0.4 percent, and the company has largely gone out of business.

Rapid Obsolescence

With the release of the iPad, and the ability of readers to download eBooks quickly and inexpensively, the entire book market changed. Within a year, Borders, one of the largest book retailers in the world, had gone bankrupt and shut down its six hundred stores. This is happening to companies in almost every industry. Because they failed to adapt their business model to the new market situation driven by the onslaught of information, technology, and competition, long-established companies quickly disappeared into the pages of business history.

Your personal business model, the way you have organized your life and career, may be partially or completely obsolete as well. And if it is not obsolete today, it will definitely be at some time in the future.

Businesses get into trouble when customer tastes and demands change. Individuals have problems in their careers when employer requirements, in terms of specialized talents, skills, and abilities, change as well. To survive and thrive today, you must be on the cutting edge, as an individual or an organization, of the changes taking place around you.

The 80/20 Rule and Income

Today, many people have obsolete skills; they are being replaced by people with better and more appropriate skills that are in higher demand. Gary Becker, the Nobel Prize–winning economist, reported in the *Wall Street Journal* about a study on income growth. What Becker found in research at the University of Chicago was that the average income of people in the bottom 80 percent increased at about 3 percent per year, just equal to or slightly ahead of the rate of inflation.

However, the incomes of people in the top 20 percent were increasing at an average of 11 percent per year, enabling them to double their income every six or seven years and move into the upper-middle class or even the wealthy classes over the course of their working lifetimes.

What was the major difference between the 20 percent and the 80 percent? It was the commitment to continuous learning and upgrading of skills. People in the top 20 percent bought all the books, attended all the courses, listened to all of the audio programs, and continually sought ways to do their jobs better, cheaper, and faster.

Unplanned Skill Obsolescence

People in the bottom 80 percent were exactly the opposite. They seldom read a book, took a course, or made any effort to upgrade their skills. They spent their spare time in activities that were tension relieving rather than goal achieving. As a result, they fell further and further behind, usually unknowingly.

When they finally lost their jobs, they found that their skill sets, largely based on experience, were of minimal value to current employers. And because continuous learning and new skill development were not part of their worldview, they simply went home and watched television. As a result, they often found themselves unemployed for months and even years.

Many people today, at all income levels and in all career categories, are unaware of this pressing need to continually upgrade their skills. But as Pat Riley, the basketball coach, said, "If you're not getting better, you're getting worse."

The Race Is On

No one stays in the same place for very long. If you are not continually upgrading your knowledge and skills, you are not staying even. You are actually falling further and further behind, while people who are aggressive about continuous learning are moving further and faster ahead.

Most people today are stuck in a rut, and the only difference between a rut and a grave is the depth. As motivational speaker Jim Rohn said, "If you're stuck in a rut, I hope a wagon wheel comes along to motivate you out of it."

The Three Enemies

Three enemies of change and flexibility must be countered head-on. The first and worst is the "comfort zone." People start doing or working at something and quickly become comfortable. They then resist any change, even positive change that requires them to do something new or different.

Instead of learning, growing, and expanding their envelope of possibilities, they dig in their heels, justify and rationalize their resistance to change, and often sabotage the change efforts of others.

In Warren Bennis's book *Leaders*, he describes how the top people in his study resisted the pull of the comfort zone by setting bigger and bigger goals for themselves and their organizations, goals that would be impossible to achieve without major changes and improvements.

In Peter Diamandis's 2015 book, *Bold*, he urges mold breakers and earth shakers to set goals to achieve ten times or one hundred times their current levels of sales, income, and profitability in the years ahead. This size of goal, which seems overwhelming at first, soon leads to expanded thinking and new ideas to "go where no man has ever gone before" (*Star Trek*).

FEAR HOLDS PEOPLE BACK

The second major obstacle to flexibility, to challenging and questioning the status quo, is fear of all kinds, but especially the fear of failure. "What if we try something new and it doesn't work?"

According to the October 2013 *Harvard Business Review*, the major obstacles to business model innovation are fear and uncertainty. Eighty percent of corporate executives rank business model innovation ahead of the development of new products and services in terms of importance. But they don't know how to do it, so they procrastinate and hope that the next generation of leaders will make the changes that will be necessary to survive and thrive.

FEELING UNABLE TO CHANGE

The third reason that people fear and resist change is "learned helplessness." The individuals responsible know that change is essential, but they feel that they are helpless, caught up in the complexities of the current situation and unable to change.

Learned helplessness is expressed in the words "I can't" or "We can't." What then follows is a litany of excuses in terms of not enough time, not enough money, not enough available talent, and other explanations for why change is not possible that involve a number of external pressures and internal limitations.

But as Winston Churchill said, "If you don't fight when you have a chance of victory, you will soon have to fight when you have no chance at all." The rule is to change when you can, not when you have to or have no other choice.

Someone should have told this to the executives at Blockbuster, a company that dominated the market for video movies to be viewed at home. When Netflix came along, the people at Blockbuster dismissed it as a small company that could never challenge the dominance of Blockbuster in the national market. But customer tastes had changed, and within a few years Netflix was the biggest player in the delivery of movies, both by mail and online, and Blockbuster was bankrupt.

Open Up Your Thinking

There are several powerful, practical thinking tools that you can use to unlock your creativity, expand your thinking, and move yourself out of the comfort zone.

The all-around champion tool to change your perspective and to develop higher levels of flexibility is "zero-based thinking."

Zero-based thinking comes from zero-based accounting. In zero-based accounting, you challenge every expense at the beginning of every accounting period. You ask not whether you should increase or decrease a particular expense but whether or not you should be spending money in this area at all.

In zero-based thinking, you ask the brutal question, "Is there anything that we are doing today that, knowing what we now know, we wouldn't start up again if we had to do it over?"

Do a KWINK Analysis

Apply a KWINK (Knowing What I Now Know) analysis to every part of your business and personal life. Is there anything that you are doing today that you wouldn't get into again, if you had to do it over, knowing what you now know?

How do you know if you are dealing with a zero-based thinking situation? Simple—the answer is stress! If there is something in your life that you wouldn't get into again today, you will continually experience stress, worry, anger, frustration, and dissatisfaction in that area or with some person. This negative situation often permeates your conversation, distracts you throughout the day, and keeps you awake at night.

Start with Your Relationships

In zero-based thinking, start with your relationships of all kinds. Is there any person in your business or personal life that you would not get involved with again if you had to do it over?

Is there anyone in your business whom you would not hire, assign or delegate tasks to, promote, or even go to work for today knowing what you now know?

If there is someone whom you would not get involved with again today, the only question is, "How do you end this situation, and how fast?"

Can you guess how many of your decisions will turn out to be wrong in the fullness of time? According to the American Management Association, fully 70 percent of decisions made in the world of work, and probably in personal life, turn out to be wrong eventually. They can be a little bit wrong, a lot wrong, or totally wrong. To develop high levels of flexibility, to perform at your best, you must be prepared to make the three statements of the superior executive.

ADMIT YOU ARE NOT PERFECT

"I was wrong." Look around you at your situation, and especially at those areas that are causing you stress, dissatisfaction, or unhappiness, and be willing to admit that you were wrong. When you made the decision or got into the situation, it seemed like the right thing to do. Based on the information you had at the time, it was quite logical. But "the answers have changed."

You have learned things that you did not know before, and the external situation and requirements have changed as well. What seemed to be the right decision when you made it has turned out to be the wrong decision today. As soon as you admit that you were wrong and take action to correct the situation, your stress evaporates.

Sometimes, people think that by admitting they are wrong, they are demonstrating weakness. They think people will not respect them if they admit that a decision they made and defended in the past was wrong. But it is exactly the opposite. In times of turbulence and rapid change, having the courage and character to admit you were wrong, when the mistake is probably clear to everyone around you, actually increases their respect for you and their willingness to be influenced by you in the future.

On the other hand, no one looks more weak and foolish than someone who is obviously wrong but refuses to admit it.

Here's an interesting point. When you identify a situation that you would not get into again today, knowing what you now know, it is too late to save the situation, or the person. It is over. The only question now is, "How much time, money, trouble, and pain are you going to lose or suffer before you admit that you were wrong and take whatever action is necessary to rectify the situation?"

Admit You Made a Mistake

"I made a mistake." Because of ego, many people find it difficult to admit that they have made a mistake, even when they obviously have, and it is clear to everyone around them. Don't let this happen to you.

Because you are going to be wrong and make mistakes fully 70 percent of the time, don't wait for everyone else to figure it out. Instead, jump ahead of the curve and quickly admit, "I was wrong. I made a mistake." And then rectify the situation as rapidly as you can.

CHANGE YOUR MIND

"I changed my mind." Again, changing your mind when you get new information is a mark of courage, character, and flexibility, not of weakness. Even if you have spent eighteen months developing a new business or product strategy, if you get new information that invalidates your key conclusions, be prepared to change your mind, to abandon the now-obsolete strategy in favor of doing something new, different, and more appropriate to the current situation.

The more readily you can say the words "I was wrong, I made a mistake, I changed my mind," the better you will think and the more respected you will be by all the people around you.

Reevaluate Your Business and Career

The second area where you apply zero-based thinking has to do with every aspect of your business and career, including and especially your business model.

Is there any product or service that, knowing what you now know, you would not bring to the current market? Is there any process, method, or expense in your business that you would not start up again today, knowing what you now know? Is there anything in your current strategy that, knowing what you now know, you would not get into again if you had it to do over?

Is there any part of your career—the work you do, the activities you engage in—that, knowing what you now know, you wouldn't get into again today? Remember, it is quite common for people to have many different jobs, in different companies and industries, using different skills, over the course of a lifetime. Many people decide to start over in a new field and learn an entirely new set of skills when the economy changes. Could this apply to you?

If the answer is yes, the next question is, "How do I get out of this situation or discontinue it, and how fast?"

Evaluate Your Investments

The third area for zero-based thinking has to do with investments, especially those of time, money, and emotion.

In accounting, there is a category called sunk costs. This is an amount of money that has been spent and is gone forever. It cannot be recouped. It is like dropping an anvil off a ship in the middle of the ocean; you can never get it back. It is gone. It is a "sunk cost."

It is amazing how many businesses and individuals are confused in this area. They are constantly trying to recover sunk costs. This is called "throwing good money after bad" or "throwing money down a rat hole."

Your Investment Is Gone Forever

This refusal to accept the fact of a sunk cost is especially true with regard to time. Is there any area of your life where you have invested a large amount of time, in a project, a service, a person, or even the development of a skill that is no longer helpful or necessary? Be prepared to recognize that this past investment of time has now become a sunk cost. Accept it. Move on. And don't invest any more time in an area where, in your heart, you know it is not the best use of your time and effort.

The second area of sunk costs has to do with invest-ments. Is there any financial investment that, knowing what you now know, you would not make again today if you had to do it over?

If there is, the next question is, "How do I get out of this investment, and how fast?"

It is sad to see how many people and companies keep investing money in an area that knowing what they now know, they would never invest in at all if they had to do it over.

Imagine Starting Over Again Today

The third area of zero-based thinking has to do with emo-tions. According to psychologists, people hate to lose time, money, or emotion of any kind. They often have a mental block about losses, refusing to admit them and attempting to recoup them in some way.

Throughout your life, you will invest a lot of emotion in people, projects, and situations. You will put your whole heart into making the situation or relationship work. But at the end of the day, you will have to admit that you were not successful. Your investment of emotion has been lost. It is gone forever. It cannot be retrieved or recouped. It is a sunk cost.

It takes tremendous character to face up to the reality of a failed situation or relationship and to admit that you were wrong, you made a mistake, and you've changed your mind. But the more often you practice zero-based thinking, the more flexible you become.

The Big Payoff

Here is the good news: When you finally have the courage to put an end to a zero-based thinking situation, you will have the same reaction that people have all over the world. First, you will feel a great sense of relief, even exhilaration, and liberation. You will feel as though a great weight has been lifted off your shoulders.

Second, you will ask yourself, "Why didn't I do this a long time ago?"

The skill of zero-based thinking is absolutely essential if you want to realize your full potential in your work and personal life. And the more you practice it, the better you get at it. Soon, you will be able to say, "There is not a situation in my life that I would change or get out of today if I had to do it over."

The Seven *R*s of Superior Thinking

Sometimes, the simplest ideas can jar your thinking and cause you to see your situation in a completely different way. The key is for you to always be open to the possibility that whatever you are doing, you could be completely wrong. There could be a completely different and better way to do almost anything, and there usually is.

There are seven tools you can use to increase your flexibility and your mental agility.

1. **Rethinking:** This requires that you stop the clock, take a time-out, and stand back to look at your situation objectively. Ask yourself three questions:

   - What am I trying to do?
   - How am I trying to do it?
   - Could there be a better way?

   Whenever you experience frustration or resistance of any kind in your attempt to achieve your goals, step back and ask yourself these three questions.

   Very often you will find that what you are trying to do is not the correct thing to do, or it is not as important as it used to be. You may find that the way you are trying to do it is not working. And by asking if there could be a better way, you open your mind to an infinite number of possibilities, because there is almost always a better way.

2. **Reevaluating:** Practice zero-based thinking, and consider the possibilities of doing things completely differently.

   Whenever you are not happy with an ongoing situation, ask yourself, "If I were not now in this situation, knowing what I now know, would I get into it again today?"

   If the answer is no, how do you get out of it, and how fast?

3. **Reorganizing:** Look for ways to increase the efficiency and effectiveness of your operations by moving people and resources around and by deploying them in different ways.

   - What are your most important goals in your work and business right now? Have they changed?
   - Who are your most important, valuable, and productive people?
   - How can you reorganize your work so that your best and most productive people are focused on

your most important goals and greatest opportunities?

4. **Restructuring:** This involves moving your people and resources into the 20 percent of activities that can account for 80 percent of your results.

   - What are the 20 percent of results that account for 80 percent of the income and profits of your business?
   - What are the top 20 percent of your activities that account for 80 percent of your total results?
   - Who are the top 20 percent of your staff who produce 80 percent of the total results?

   In business, your primary concern should be revenue generation. Move your very best people into those areas where they can have the greatest positive effect on generating more revenue for your company.

5. **Reengineering:** Continually seek ways to simplify your work and life by delegating, outsourcing, downsizing, or eliminating certain activities.

   - What activities or processes can you simplify and streamline so they can be done faster and with less time and money?

- What activities can you delegate to others or outsource to specialist companies?
- What activities could you eliminate altogether with no real loss of productivity, sales, or profitability?

Each time you ask one of these questions, you will stimulate your creativity and get answers that you can apply to streamline your business and get more and better results, faster and cheaper.

6. **Reinventing:** Continually imagine what you would do differently if you were starting over again today.

- Imagine starting your business or department over again today. What would you do differently?
- What would you do more of?
- What would you do less of?
- What would you start doing that you are not doing right now?
- What would you stop doing altogether?

These questions will give you ideas and insights every time you ask them. What should you do more of, less of, start, or stop?

---

7. **Regaining control:** This requires that you take specific action in your work and business based on your answers to the prior six Rs.

- What one action are you going to take immediately regarding your own personal work and activities?
- What one action are you going to take immediately regarding your staff?
- What one action are you going to take immediately regarding the business itself?

In each case, imagine that you have no limits. Imagine that you have all the time and money, all the talents and abilities, all the friends and contacts, and all the resources you need to be, do, or have anything in your business or personal life.

Your main job is to become absolutely clear about the right thing, the best thing, to do and then to commit wholeheartedly to the new course of action.

◈◈

ACTION EXERCISES

1. Examine your personal and corporate business model. Ask yourself if there could be a better way for you to generate sales, profitability, and personal income.

2. Apply the KWINK analysis to every part of your business and personal life. "Knowing what I now know, is there anything that I am doing that I would not get into again today if I had it to do over?"

3. What should you do more of, less of, start, or stop altogether to get different and better results?

8

Creative Thinking Versus
Mechanical Thinking

The imagination is literally the workshop wherein are fashioned
all plans created by man.

—NAPOLEON HILL

CREATIVE THINKERS rule the world! They are continually
seeking faster, better, and easier ways to accomplish goals
that are important to other people. They practice the CANEI
principle, which stands for "Continuous and Never-Ending
Improvement."

They are responsible for all of the great breakthroughs,
innovations, and progress in human history. They know that
sometimes one good idea is all it takes to change the course
of a business or an individual life.

Mechanical Thinking

Mechanical thinking, on the other hand, tends to be rigid and inflexible. It is "my way or the highway." Mechanical thinking is rooted in fears of failure or making a mistake and losing time, money, or both. It is triggered by fears of criticism or disapproval, trying something that doesn't work.

Poor thinkers think in terms of black and white rather than shades of gray. They think in extremes of yes versus no, up versus down. They think there is only one way when there are usually many ways. In the face of change and confrontation, they develop psychosclerosis, which is defined as a "hardening of the attitudes."

They are victims of "homeostasis," a striving for constancy. They are stuck in their comfort zones. They resent and fear anything new or different, even an improvement in conditions. But this is not for you.

You Are a Potential Genius

You have more creative potential than you could use in a hundred lifetimes. The more of your creative ability you use, the more you can use. You actually become more creative each time you come up with something new. It is said that every child is born a genius, and this means you, throughout your lifetime.

It turns out that creativity is the single best indicator or predictor of success in life and in work. The more creative you are, the more and better ideas you will come up with to improve your life, work, and everything around you. One good idea can be enough to change the entire direction of your life.

How do you recognize creativity? Creative people are curious. They ask a lot of questions and are never satisfied. In fact, you can become more creative just by asking more questions about the things going on around you and not being content with superficial answers.

Genius Throughout the Ages

There are many studies of the qualities of geniuses throughout the ages. The first fact they discovered was that intelligence was not a matter of IQ or academic qualifications. Many so-called geniuses had average or slightly above-average intelligence. Genius or excellent thinking was instead more a matter of attitude and approach toward the inevitable challenges of life.

It appears that geniuses develop three qualities over time.

KEEP AN OPEN MIND

First, they approach every problem or situation with an open mind, almost a childlike attitude of exploration and discovery. The more open your mind is to completely new and different approaches to any situation in your life, the more likely it is that you are going to get insights and ideas that move you out of your comfort zone—that enable you to think outside the box. They continually ask "Why?" and "Why not?" and "What if?"

Second, geniuses carefully consider every aspect of a problem, refusing to jump to conclusions, gathering more and more data instead. They test and validate their tentative conclusions at each stage. They avoid a rush to judgment. They are always open to the possibility that they could be wrong, or that their idea is no good.

THE BEST SOLUTION

Albert Einstein was once asked, "If there was a major emergency or potential disaster that was going to destroy the earth in 60 minutes, and you were asked to find a solution, what would you do?"

Einstein replied, "I would spend the first 59 minutes

gathering information, and the last minute solving the problem in the best possible way."

In business today, especially in new product development, the more time you spend working closely with customers to be sure that your new product or service idea is exactly what they want, need, and are willing to pay for, the more likely it is that you will be successful in a fast-changing and highly competitive market.

THE SYSTEMATIC APPROACH

Third, geniuses of all kinds use a systematic approach to problem solving and decision making. Accomplished mathematicians, physicists, doctors, mechanics, and people in other professions do not throw themselves at a problem like a dog chasing a passing car. Rather, they follow a carefully designed checklist and work their way through a problem, step by step, toward a conclusion.

Atul Gawande, in his book *The Checklist Manifesto*, tells the story of two investment experts, both successful, but one far more successful than the other.

It turned out that they both had many years of experience in evaluating and making substantial investments for themselves and their clients. But the more successful adviser had developed a checklist of essential questions to ask and tests to apply to an investment proposal before making a decision.

The other adviser used many of the same techniques and tactics to appraise an investment, but he operated more from intuition and experience. As a result, he often lost money when he shouldn't have.

Here was the interesting point that Gawande made. The first adviser was consistently more successful than the second. But on various occasions, he made mistakes and lost money. The reason was invariably the same. He had neglected to follow his own checklist. He had missed one or two vital points in his list of important considerations. When he went back to following his checklist meticulously, his investment record improved significantly.

The Systematic Problem-Solving Method

Here is a structured/unstructured way of problem solving and decision making developed by experts and think tanks over the years. I have synthesized the best ideas I have discovered into a single simple method that you can use for the rest of your career.

STEP ONE: Define the problem or goal clearly, in writing, on the page in front of you. If you are working with a group, write and rewrite the problem or goal on a flip chart or a whiteboard until everyone agrees, "Yes. This is the correct definition of the problem."

In medicine, they say, "Accurate diagnosis is half the cure."

In business, developing the correct definition of the problem often makes the solution appear obvious.

STEP TWO: Once you have defined the problem or goal clearly, you ask, "What else is the problem?"

Beware of any problem for which there is only one definition. Define and redefine the problem several different ways to make it more amenable to the correct solution. (Note: It may be not a problem at all but rather an opportunity.)

The worst thing you can do is to come up with a great solution to the wrong problem or to a problem that does not exist.

Product Failure Rates

Fully 80 percent of new products and services fail within twelve months. The primary reason for this is that companies develop a product that solves a problem that customers don't have.

It is like the story of the dog food company that invested many millions of dollars developing the perfect dog food—nutritionally balanced in every way. But the product failed in the marketplace. When the product developers were asked what had happened, they replied, "The problem was that the dogs hated it."

Whatever definition of the problem that you settle on

is going to determine the direction of the solution. If your problem definition is incorrect, your solution, however brilliant, won't work.

Sales Improvement Process

In my work with sales organizations, I take them through a systematic process of creative thinking. In almost every case, the number one problem that a business faces is low sales. So I start off with a question, "What is the problem?"

The first definition of the problem is usually "Our sales are too low."

What else is the problem?
We are not attracting enough new customers.

What else is the problem?
The customers that we do attract are not buying enough.

What else is the problem?
We are not converting enough of our prospects into paying customers.

What else is the problem?
Our advertising and promotion are not attracting enough new customers.

What else is the problem?

Our customers are not buying often enough.

What else is the problem?

Our customers are buying too much from our competitors.

Keep asking the "what else" question until you find the correct definition of the problem.

The Definition Determines the Solution

Whichever of these answers that you decide upon—if it is the correct problem—requires a different, and sometimes a completely different, solution. This is why it is so important that you test and validate your answer to be sure you are working on the right problem in the first place.

STEP THREE: You ask, "What is the solution to our problem?" Whatever answer you come up with, you then ask, "What else is the solution to our problem?"

Beware of a problem for which there is only one solution. There is a direct relationship between the number of possible solutions you develop and the quality of the final solution you settle upon. Very often, two unrealistic ideas combined could turn out to be one brilliant idea that changes the direction of your business.

STEP FOUR: Once you have developed a wide range of possible solutions, you must narrow them down and make a decision. In most cases, any decision is better than no decision at all. If you cannot make a decision immediately, set a deadline by which you will make your decision and take action.

Steve Jobs once said, "Creative ideas come from connecting the dots in a different way." Here is the key used by superior thinkers everywhere: If you are struggling with a decision, collect more dots. Get more information. Hire a consultant who specializes in this area. Don't be cheap in collecting the best information possible. One new or unconsidered idea can make or save you a fortune.

STEP FIVE: Determine how you will measure the success of this decision. Set clear measures and benchmarks. Quantify your desired results. The rule is this: "If you want to succeed in business, set measures for everything. If you want to get rich, set financial measures for everything."

Remember, if you can't measure it, you can't manage it. And what gets measured gets done.

STEP SIX: Assign responsibility for the project, task, or subtask to a specific person or persons.

Every product, service, or project needs a champion, someone who is completely in charge of the project and whose personal success, pay, and promotion are determined or strongly affected by the results.

A major mistake that small and large companies make is that they agree on a new product or service idea, or on a project of some kind, and then everyone goes back to work. No one is assigned specific responsibility for this project. It then becomes an "orphan project" in the company—something that belongs to everyone and to no one. Don't let this happen in your business.

STEP SEVEN: Set a deadline and sub-deadlines for completion. The more important the potential result, the more often and more accurately you must manage and measure progress. Inspect what you expect. What gets inspected gets done.

STEP EIGHT: Develop a Plan B, a fallback plan or an alternative in case your first solution does not work for any reason. Fill out the "Disaster Report." Ask, "What is the worst possible thing that could happen in this situation?"

The worst possible outcome is that it could fail completely, and all the time and money invested will be lost.

How could you minimize the possibilities of failure? How could you maximize the possibilities of success? What will you do if your solution doesn't work?

Develop a Fallback Plan

Great generals plan to win every battle, but they prepare for defeat if it occurs. They set aside reserves of men and ammunition. They develop a contingency or fallback plan. They know that an orderly retreat is better than a complete rout.

Never "bet the ranch" on a new course of action. Only take calculated risks—risks that you can bounce back from if they fail completely.

Hope is not a strategy; it is a formula for disaster. In business, the new product idea of "build it and they will come" is almost a surefire recipe for failure.

STEP NINE: Take action on your idea. Move fast. Develop a sense of urgency. Do something. Do anything. But get on with it, as quickly as possible.

General George Patton said, "A good plan violently executed *now* is better than a perfect plan next week."

Apply this systematic method of problem solving to each problem or obstacle your business faces, disciplining yourself to follow the recipe for superior thinking. You will be happily surprised at the result.

Solution-Focused Thinking Versus Problem-Focused Thinking

The true mark of your intelligence and your creativity is your ability to solve problems and make decisions. Whatever title is written on your business card, your true job description is "problem solver." From the time you start work in the morning until the time you quit for the day, and afterward, you are solving problems, small and large, all day long.

General Colin Powell said, "Leadership is the ability to solve problems."

Success is the ability to solve problems as well. A goal or an objective unachieved, in any area, is merely a problem unsolved. This is why a systematic approach to problem solving, one that works at a higher level and more consistently, is absolutely vital for you to achieve the maximum success that is possible for you.

Think About Solutions

As it happens, successful people think about solutions most of the time. Unsuccessful people think about problems most of the time. Successful people think about how to solve the problem or remove the obstacle and what actions can be taken immediately to improve the situation.

Unsuccessful people think about the problem and who is to blame. They allow themselves to become angry and upset about a problem that occurs or an obstacle that arises. This triggers negative thinking, anger, and the search for the guilty party—"Who did it?" But it does nothing to help them find the solution.

Unlock Your Creative Powers

There are three keys to unlocking your creative powers that we have spoken about before. They are clarity, focus, and concentration.

First, you must be clear about the goal but flexible about the process of achieving it. Keep an open mind. Be willing to consider a variety of different ways to achieve the same result.

Second, focus. Bring all of your brainpower, and that of others, to focus like a laser beam on a single problem, obstacle, or difficulty, without diversion or distraction. Stay on one subject at a time.

Third, concentration. Put aside everything else, and concentrate 100 percent until you have solved your biggest problem or achieved your most important goal.

Jim Collins, in his book *Good to Great*, tells the story of the fox and the hedgehog, which comes from an essay by Isaiah Berlin. He says that the fox is very clever and knows many things. But the hedgehog is more successful because he knows one big thing.

Clarity, focus, and concentration enable you to bring all your mental powers to bear on solving one big problem or achieving one big goal.

The Attraction of Distraction

In our modern world of computers and e-mail, perhaps the greatest enemy is the "attraction of distraction," chasing after the shiny objects of immediate stimulus—e-mail, text messages, phone calls, and social media—all of which cause your mind to scatter and disrupt your ability to focus and concentrate.

According to *USA Today,* continuously responding to electronic interruptions, especially e-mail and text messages, burns up your brain fuel, glucose, at a rapid rate. The average adult checks his or her e-mail all day long and is constantly distracted, like an attention deficit disorder dog, by signals and alarms on e-mail and smartphones.

As a result, the average e-mail-addicted employee loses ten full IQ points each day, becoming dumber by the hour. By the end of the day, many people are burned out, unable to concentrate or make even the simplest of decisions. And they are further and further behind on their key tasks.

Multitasking Versus Task Switching

Constantly responding to e-mails, text messages, and phone calls forces the individual to engage in what is called multitasking. However, this is more rightly defined as task switching. You are not doing several tasks; instead, you are switching back and forth, from one task to another and then back again. According to one study, it takes you about seventeen minutes after you have broken off a task to respond to an incoming message for you to get back "on task" again.

Throughout the day, your attention switches back and forth, like a windshield wiper, seldom completing anything of value. When you add in social media and the obsession that many people have with checking Facebook, Twitter, and LinkedIn, you have a formula for career disaster. This is why they say, "Social networking is social not working."

The solution is simple. Leave things off. Check your e-mail twice a day, at 11:00 a.m. and at 3:00 p.m. Other than that, turn everything off so that you can dedicate yourself single-mindedly to the task at hand.

The Principle of Constraints

This is one of the best creative thinking tools of all. The Principle of Constraints says that between you and any goal there is a constraint that determines how fast you achieve that goal.

Sometimes this is called the bottleneck. Sometimes it is referred to as the choke point. Andrew Grove, the former CEO of Intel, referred to the main constraint holding you back as the "limiting factor" in any production process.

What is your major goal today, and what is the constraint that sets the speed at which you achieve it?

To rephrase this question, "Why aren't you already at your goal?"

If your goal is to increase your sales and profitability by 50 percent, why aren't your sales and profitability already 50 percent higher? If your goal is to lose weight, why aren't you already at your ideal weight? When you ask this question, very often the answer you come up with is the constraint that is holding you back. Often, when you ask and answer this question, what will pop into your mind will be your favorite excuses, the reasons that you most commonly give for nonachievement in a particular area.

Identify the Limiting Factor

In each situation, your first job is to identify this limiting factor and then focus single-mindedly on alleviating it. This way of thinking and acting can move you toward your goals faster than almost anything else you can do.

The 80/20 rule applies to constraints in your personal and business life. Fully 80 percent of the factors that are holding you back from achieving your most important goals are within yourself or within your business. Only 20 percent are on the outside, external to you and your business.

When you begin identifying and removing constraints, always start with yourself. Ask the key question, "What is it in me (or in my business) that is holding me back from achieving my goal?"

Remember, the natural tendency of most people is to blame their problems on external forces and other people. The hallmark of superior thinkers is that they accept complete responsibility for any problem or difficulty and then they look into themselves for what is setting the speed at which they achieve the goal they desire.

What-If Thinking

One of the most powerful questions you can ask in triggering creativity is, "What if?" Each time you ask this question, you break the bonds of limited thinking that may keep you working in a narrow area, and you open your mind to more and more possibilities.

What-if thinking is considered the breakthrough concept that made Federal Express one of the most successful companies in the world. It started by asking, "What if it was possible to deliver a letter overnight, anywhere in the country?"

When Fred Smith, founder, chairman, president, and CEO of FedEx, suggested this idea in an undergraduate term paper at Yale, his professor gave him a C, saying that the idea was not very realistic. At that time, first-class mail in the United States took anywhere from three to five days, and sometimes longer, to reach its destination. The idea of overnight mail delivery seemed highly improbable.

Break the Barriers

By continually asking "What if?" Fred Smith and the executives of FedEx were able to develop creative ideas that not only achieved the goal but led to one of the largest and most successful companies in the world.

"What if it was possible to put the keyboard on the screen of a cell phone?" (Apple, now the largest company in the world.)

"What if we could sell and deliver almost any book by e-mail and direct home delivery?" (Amazon.com, now the biggest vendor of books in the world.)

"What if we could put a man on the moon and bring him safely back to earth?" (John F. Kennedy—1962.)

When President John F. Kennedy asked the scientist in charge of the American space program, Wernher von Braun, what it would take to put a man on the moon and bring him back safely, von Braun replied simply, "The will to do it."

In many situations, in your business and personal life, what is most required for success is simply "the will to do it."

My friend Joel Weldon was famous for his talk "Success Comes in Cans, Not in Cannots." It is the same with you.

The Process of Innovation

The philosophy of every successful business and successful executive is CANEI, which, as said above, stands for "Continuous and Never-Ending Improvement."

Resolve to move boldly out of your comfort zone. Continually search for newer, better, faster, and cheaper ways to achieve your goals and to move ahead. Be prepared to fail over and over again when you are developing or introducing new products, services, methods, or strategies. Nothing ever works out the way you think it will. You will experience constant frustrations, difficulties, setbacks, and temporary failures on the way to success.

Thomas J. Watson Sr., the founder of IBM, was once asked how to succeed faster. He replied, "If you want to succeed faster, you must double your rate of failure. Success lies on the far side of failure."

In fact, there is no such thing as failure. There is only feedback. Difficulties come not to obstruct but to instruct.

The formula has always been "Try, try again, and then try something else."

Your ability to solve problems, make decisions, and find creative, innovative ways to grow your business, increase your sales, and boost your profits is the ultimate key to your success.

⚡

ACTION EXERCISES

1. Select one problem that you or your business is wrestling with today and put it through the systematic method of problem solving. It could change your future.

2. Identify one goal that you have and determine the biggest constraint, the limiting factor that sets the speed at which you achieve that goal. What could you do to alleviate this constraint?

3. Select one product or service you offer and develop as many ways as possible to make it better, faster, or cheaper for your customers.

9

Entrepreneurial Thinking Versus Corporate Thinking

Be true to the best you know. This is your high ideal. If you do
your best, you cannot do more.

—H. W. DRESSER

ALL PEOPLE WANT to achieve the highest possible level of
financial success in the course of their careers. According to
Thomas Stanley, author of *The Millionaire Next Door*, fully
80 percent of self-made millionaires are entrepreneurs. They
earned their fortunes in one lifetime by starting and building their own business, by producing and selling something
to someone. They thought and acted like entrepreneurs most
of the time.

According to the March 2015 *Forbes* magazine, there are
1,826 billionaires in the world today, 66 percent of whom
are self-made. They started as entrepreneurs with nothing
and built their fortunes from the ground up by creating and

selling products and services that people wanted and were willing to buy and pay for.

Think About Customers

Entrepreneurial thinking means focusing on the customers at all times, thinking about the customers continually.

Tom Peters wrote in the book *In Search of Excellence* that the single most important quality of successful businesses was "an obsession with customer service."

Not long ago, I spent a day with the president of a $2 billion company that he had started at his kitchen table. When I asked him what position he saw himself as having in his business, he immediately replied, "Chief Sales Officer." He said, "This was my position when we started, and it is still my position today. I think about sales all the time."

Corporate Thinking

Corporate thinking is different from entrepreneurial thinking. Company people, whether employees, managers, executives, or technicians, view customers either with disinterest or as problems who are always complaining or requesting something new or different. Customers are often seen as flies that have to be swatted and brushed away.

Corporate thinkers are preoccupied with doing their jobs,

pleasing their superiors, following the rules, and doing the minimum necessary to avoid being fired or laid off. Employees who are corporate types use the pronouns "them, they, and their" to describe the company and the people in charge.

They feel that whatever happens in the company has little to do with them personally. They say, "A job is a job." As one corporate type told me some time ago, "When I go to work, I think about my job, but when I come home, I don't think about my job or company at all."

Lack of Engagement

Many researchers conclude that more than 60 percent of employees at large and small companies are "disengaged." They feel no deep commitment or loyalty to the company. They are just going through the motions of work, thinking about doing something else. They check the want ads on a regular basis, post their résumés and qualifications on Craigslist, LinkedIn, and other Web sites, and are continually looking for something else to do.

Corporate types come to work at the last minute, take every minute of coffee breaks and lunches, and spend as much as 50 percent of their time chitchatting with co-workers, checking their e-mail, and doing things of no or low value to their company.

Commitment Is the Key

Entrepreneurial thinkers are different. They are committed to the success of the company. They see themselves as self-employed and act as if they owned their companies personally.

They use words like "we," "mine," and "our" when they refer to their company and to their products and services. Above all, they accept and take on high levels of responsibility for results.

Entrepreneurial thinkers are always volunteering for more responsibility. They continually think about making a greater contribution. They are continually upgrading their skills, learning new things, and seeking ways to become more valuable to their companies.

Above all, entrepreneurial thinkers search for ways to increase the sales and profitability of their companies.

Entrepreneurial thinking is customer-centric, customer-focused thinking. Entrepreneurial thinkers think about customers all the time.

Sales Are Central

As we said in a previous chapter, the number one reason for business success is high sales. The number one reason for business failure is low sales. All else is commentary.

The key to business success is SMS, which stands for "Sell More Stuff." This is what the entrepreneurial thinker focuses on most of the time. How can we sell more stuff?

Successful businesspeople have certain qualities, characteristics, and disciplines that enable them to achieve far more than the average person.

There are several ways for you to develop the qualities of entrepreneurial thinking and to make a greater contribution to the sales and profitability of your organization. Remember the three keys: clarity, focus, and concentration.

Ask the Basic Questions

There are basic business questions that you need to ask and answer all the time, especially when you face rapid change in knowledge, technology, and competition.

First, what business are you really in? Define your business in terms of how you serve your customers, the improvements or transformations your products bring about in their lives and work.

Corporate thinkers see their businesses as organizations that produce and sell products and services. Entrepreneurial thinkers see their business mission as enhancing and enriching the lives of their customers.

Try to describe your business in terms of the positive change or improvement your products or services make in your customers' lives without mentioning your company, products, or services. This can be a real challenge the first time you try it.

Think Like a Customer

The corporate type says, "I sell cars."

The entrepreneur says, "I enable people to drive wherever they want in comfort and safety."

You will know when you are describing your product or service in terms of the job that it does for your customers, the problems that it solves, and the benefits that your customers enjoy, because you will trigger the response "How do you do that?" or "I want that!" or "That's for me!"

Who is your ideal customer, the perfect person for what you sell? This is a description of the demographics and psychographics of the type of person who most appreciates and values the special features, benefits, and results of the product or service that you offer.

What does your ideal customer consider valuable? What

is so important to him or her that you can provide that makes your prices seem unimportant?

The main reason that businesses fail is that there is little or no demand for their product. People don't value it or want it and have no interest in buying it.

Your Area of Excellence

What is it that you do especially well? What is your area of excellence or superiority in comparison to your competitors relative to what your ideal customer wants, needs, and is willing to pay for?

All companies, products, and services must have a competitive, comparative advantage over their competitors that makes them the best choice and ideally the "only" choice in their market. What is yours? What could it be?

Jack Welch said, "If you don't have competitive advantage, don't compete." He is famous for his rule that General Electric would be number one or number two in every market it was in, or it would abandon that market and concentrate its efforts somewhere else.

For a company to be successful, it must dominate a market niche. In at least one area, it must be recognized by customers in the marketplace as being "the best" for that particular customer.

In what areas do you or could you dominate your market?

What would you have to do more or less of? What would you have to start or stop doing altogether?

Peter Drucker, an adviser to Jack Welch, said, "If you don't have a clear competitive advantage, develop one."

Entrepreneurial thinking at its core is focused on developing and maintaining a meaningful competitive advantage in competitive markets.

Your Business Model

Today, the entrepreneurial focus is more and more on the business model, the complex strategy that your company uses to produce, sell, and deliver your product or service to more and more customers in a profitable and cost-effective way. What is yours?

According to Geoffrey Colvin of *Fortune* magazine, many if not most companies are operating on an old business model, one that is partially or totally obsolete.

How do you know if you have the correct business model for your business? The easiest measure is that your sales and profitability are increasing steadily and predictably.

If your sales are erratic or inconsistent, have leveled off, or, even worse, are declining, it could be that your business model no longer works. If this is the case, and you do not change your business model, the end is in sight.

Thinking About Your Business

Entrepreneurial thinking requires that you continually review and evaluate the essential elements of your business model.

1. What value does your product offer? What job does your product do for your customer? What problem does it solve? What benefits does it deliver? What pain does it take away? What goals does it enable your customers to achieve? And especially, how important are your key benefits to your customers?

    Your ability to ask and answer these questions accurately will largely determine the future of your business.

2. Who is your customer? Who are the customers who can most benefit from the products or services you offer? What are their demographics? What are their ages, incomes, education levels, genders, occupations, and type of family formation?

    What are their psychographics? What are their hopes, dreams, fears, ambitions, and aspirations relative to what you sell?

    Especially, what are their ethnographics? How do they use your product or service? What role does it play in their lives or work? How important is it to them in comparison with other things?

3. What are the most effective ways that you can market (attract new customers), sell (convert them into buyers), and distribute (get your product into the hands of your customers)?

   How could you attract more and better-paying customers? How could you sell faster and more effectively to the prospects you attract? How could you distribute your product faster and more efficiently? (Think Amazon.com!)

   The rule is that whatever you are doing today, you will have to be much, much better a year from now just to stay even in your current market.

4. How do you give such good customer service that your happy customers buy from you again and again and tell others to buy from you as well?

5. What is the cost structure of your business, and how could you change it to achieve greater profitability?

   How could you outsource, downsize, or eliminate certain activities so that you can offer the same high level of quality but at a lower cost of operations?

Continue to Question

Entrepreneurs in all types of businesses think about these critical factors all the time. They are always willing to consider the possibility that they could be wrong or that there are better ways to get results in one or more of these areas.

Entrepreneurs practice zero-based thinking continually in every area. They ask, "Is there anything that we are doing that, knowing what we now know, we wouldn't get into or start up today?"

Entrepreneurs are more concerned with what's right rather than with who's right. They keep their egos out of the discussion.

Entrepreneurs are willing to admit, "I could be wrong."

Entrepreneurs openly admit, "I made a mistake," and then they get busy correcting the mistake as quickly as possible, rather than trying to bluff, bluster, stonewall, or hope that it will go away.

With new information, entrepreneurs readily say, "I've changed my mind." They quickly embrace new ideas and methods to get better results, no matter the source.

Customer Focus

Entrepreneurial thinking requires that you think about the customer all the time. You continually seek new, different, better, faster, and cheaper ways to serve customers and give them more and more of what they really want and need.

Your ability to think like an entrepreneur rather than an employee will do more to liberate your full potential in your career than any other single factor. It might even make you rich.

ACTION EXERCISES

1. Define your perfect customer clearly. How could you serve him or her better than your competitors?
2. Determine your value offering, the one or two qualities of your products or services that make them superior to those of your competitors.
3. Examine your business model to be sure that the way you are generating sales and profitability today is the best and most efficient way to do it.

10

Rich Thinking Versus Poor Thinking

Thought is the original source of all wealth, all success, all material gain, all great discoveries and inventions, and of all achievement.

—CLAUDE M. BRISTOL

THERE HAVE NEVER BEEN more opportunities for you to become wealthy, and more different ways to achieve it, than exist today. More people are starting more businesses in more different industries than ever before. More knowledge, information, and technology are creating more products and services that people want, need, and are willing to pay for. One new idea is all you need to start a fortune.

In the year 1900, there were 5,000 millionaires in America, after almost two hundred years of economic development and growth. By the year 1980, there were 1 million millionaires in America. In 2015, there are more than 10 million millionaires and 1,826 billionaires, most of whom started with nothing and earned all their money in one lifetime. And within reason, so can you.

As Within, So Without

The Law of Correspondence works for everyone at all times under all circumstances. This law says that your outer world will be a reflection of your inner world. Everything moves from within to without. You cannot accomplish something on the outside until you first accomplish it on the inside. To be wealthy on the outside, you must think like a rich person on the inside. There is no other way.

Poor people think like poor people. They have self-limiting beliefs that hold them back and stop them from even trying. In a study completed a few years ago entitled One Hundred Million Millionaires, the authors demonstrated that if you simply saved $100 per month throughout your working lifetime, invested it, and let it grow with compound interest, it would amount to $1 million by the time you retired. Why doesn't everyone do this? Poor thinking!

Tony Robbins, in his 2014 book, *Money: Master the Game*, emphasizes what Einstein said: "Compounding is the most powerful force in the universe."

After extensive interviews with fifty of the richest people in the world, Robbins concluded that almost anyone can start small, save and invest regularly, use the miracle of compound interest, and eventually become financially independent, if not wealthy. This simple method has worked for almost everyone at all times throughout history. And it can work for you.

Self-Made Millionaires

Some years ago, I was asked to give a talk on self-made millionaires to a large group composed of business owners from all over the country. This invitation forced me to do some serious thinking. This thinking changed my life.

From the time I was a teenager, my ambition had been to be a millionaire by the age of thirty. When I reached thirty and was still broke, I put it off to thirty-five. At thirty-five, I put it off to forty, but with less and less hope that I would ever achieve that magic number.

But when I was asked to give the talk on self-made millionaires, I realized that I knew very little about them. I therefore threw my whole heart into researching who they were and what they did to get from zero to $1 million in one lifetime.

With these findings, I developed a program called 21 Success Secrets of Self-Made Millionaires, which I have presented to probably a million people in fifty countries over the years. The interesting thing was that as I researched and taught people the ways that self-made millionaires think and act, I began practicing the same principles myself. Within five years, I was a millionaire.

Reprogram Your Thinking

Many people, from all over the world, have told me that by listening to this program over and over and practicing the principles it teaches, they became millionaires as well, even after years of poverty and struggle. And so can you.

In this chapter, I am going to share with you a series of simple ideas that you can learn and apply, based on extensive research into the lives and habits of thousands of wealthy people.

By the Law of Cause and Effect, if you think and do the same things that wealthy people do, you will soon get the same results that they do.

The bestselling author Og Mandino once told me, "There are no secrets of success. There are simply timeless truths and universal principles that have been discovered and rediscovered throughout human history. All you have to do is to learn and practice them to enjoy all the success that you could desire."

Reasons People Don't Become Wealthy

Once I passed the magic million-dollar mark, I began looking around me and asking the question, "Why is it that everyone doesn't use these simple principles to become wealthy?"

As I continued my research, I found that there were seven reasons why people don't become wealthy. Let us deal with each of them in turn.

1. It Never Occurs to Them

It never occurs to them that they can become wealthy. Because of their upbringing and early conditioning, perhaps coming from a home where no one had ever been wealthy, and associating with poor people, they never thought that they too could become wealthy, just as millions of others have done before them.

2. They Never Decide to Do It

Many people wish, hope, dream, and fantasize about how their lives would be different if they had a lot of money. They admire and envy people around them who are doing better than they are. They worry about money all the time.

But they never make a firm, do-or-die decision to become wealthy. As a result, they never even take the first step. They don't learn wealth-creation techniques. They don't upgrade their knowledge and skills so that they become more valuable at their work. They make excuses and rationalize their situations by saying that success is simply a matter of "luck" and they didn't get any.

3. THEY PROCRASTINATE

If it does occur to them, and they decide to become wealthy, they never get started. They procrastinate. They move to that wonderful fantasy place called "Someday I'll."

"Someday I'll save my money rather than spending it all."

"Someday I'll upgrade my knowledge and skills."

"Someday I'll work harder and make myself more valuable."

"Someday I'll get out of debt."

They end up living on "Someday I'll" for most of their lives.

One of the great secrets of success is for you to "vote yourself off the island!" Stop making excuses and start making progress.

4. THEY FEAR FAILURE

Because of destructive criticism in early childhood and mistakes they have made as adults, they are paralyzed by the fear of making a mistake, of losing their time or money. Even if they are presented with an opportunity, they go into a form of paralysis.

Their fear of failure causes them to create all kinds of reasons not to take action. They don't have the time. They can't make the minimum investment. They don't have the necessary knowledge and skills. Like a deer caught in the headlights, they are paralyzed by the idea of failure, which causes them to never take any action at all.

As it happens, most fortunes in America were started by the sale of personal services. The people had no money, but they had the ability to work hard, to upgrade their skills, and to become more and more valuable. As a result, more and more doors of opportunity opened up for them.

5. THEY FEAR CRITICISM AND DISAPPROVAL

Many people think that if they set a goal to better themselves financially, the people around them will ridicule them and criticize them. They're afraid that those people will watch over their shoulders and gleefully point out all the mistakes they make. Because they fear the disapproval of others so much, they often attempt nothing at all.

Here's the solution. When you decide to become wealthy, don't tell anyone. Keep it a secret. Go to work on your goal privately, and only tell people when they see your life improving and ask you how you did it.

6. THEY STOP LEARNING AND GROWING

To achieve something you've never achieved before, you must learn and practice something that you've never done before. The rungs on the ladder to financial success are knowledge and skill. To be financially successful starting from nothing, you are going to have to learn, develop, and practice an entire series of new skills that will enable you to become valuable and even indispensable in your work.

Abraham Lincoln once said, "I will study and prepare myself and someday my chance will come." When you study and prepare yourself, by some universal principle, you always get an opportunity to practice your new skills. But it is up to you to develop them in the first place and to continue to develop them throughout your lifetime.

7. THEY LACK PERSISTENCE

Most people don't persist long enough to succeed. Successful people will tell you that the major reason for their success was that they refused to quit. They refused to give up when the going got tough. They persisted over and over again, year after year, even in the face of complete bankruptcy and financial ruin. They never stopped.

It is amazing how many people give up and quit working just a few steps away from the key turning point in their lives, after which they would have been a big success. Persistence and determination are the ultimate guarantors that you will achieve all your financial goals.

Learning and Practice

Fortunately, each of these limitations to financial success can be overcome through learning and practice. Each of these obstacles can be turned into a stepping-stone to success when you learn how to think the way rich people think.

The Law of Correspondence is an immutable mental law. It works, for all people, under all situations and circumstances. It is inevitable and almost completely predictable.

With regard to wealth accumulation, this law says that you will behave on the outside consistent with the thoughts, feelings, beliefs, ideas, and values that you have on the inside. You always act on the outside consistent with the way you truly believe on the inside, and if you do, you will soon get the same results and outcomes as other people who believe the same way.

As a Man Thinketh

Psychologists call this your self-concept, and it is considered the single biggest breakthrough in human potential development in the twentieth century. Your self-concept is the way you think, your bundle of beliefs about yourself. You always act on the outside consistent with your self-concept, whatever it is. And you can always tell what people think, feel, and believe about themselves by looking at what they do in their day-to-day lives.

All improvements in external performance and results begin with an improvement in your self-concept. When you start to think of yourself in positive, constructive, and financially successful ways on the inside, you begin to act consistent with those beliefs on the outside until they eventually become your reality.

Children brought up in affluent homes, especially by parents who started as entrepreneurs and who worked hard and became successful in one generation, are much more likely to become successful and wealthy as adults. Throughout their upbringing, they were surrounded by and inculcated with the beliefs and lifestyles of success and affluence. When they grow up, they expect nothing less for themselves and will accept nothing less until they achieve it.

Develop a Wealthy Mind-Set

The development of a wealthy self-concept usually requires many years of immersion and exposure to the habits and behaviors of wealthy people. But sometimes it can be a single exposure to an influential person—at a seminar, in a book, or on an audio program—that makes such a vivid impression on the individual that forever after she thinks about herself as a financial success just looking for a place to happen.

Many people have become wealthy after listening to just one audio program or attending one seminar. In many cases, the ideas and encouragement contained in a single book have set people off in a different direction that led to their achieving wealth, sometimes in just a few years.

The Historical Source of Wealth

Throughout much of human history, and still today in some countries, people acquired wealth by taking it away from someone else or from some other country. The first thing the Napoleonic armies did when they overran a country or principality was to loot that area of everything that could be carried away, sending it back to Paris. Napoleon was so accomplished at the acquisition of plunder for France that he was eventually made emperor and given unlicensed authority to send his armies out to loot all of Europe.

The first thing the Nazis did under Hitler when they overran a country was to steal everything that could be moved and send it back to Germany by the trainload. When the Russians counterattacked in World War II, they looted and plundered everything in their path. Throughout history, every dictator who comes to power in any country immediately steals everything he can get his hands on. Wealth was not created in these cases; it was transferred from the weaker to the stronger.

Wealth Creation Today

Then, after 1815 in Europe, and eventually in America, a phenomenon occurred that had never been seen in human history. People found that they could create wealth by producing products and services that other people wanted, needed, and were willing to pay for. Legal systems were set up to protect the production and acquisition of wealth in this way, thereby enriching every country that embraced a market system.

Because entrepreneurs and business builders did not fear that their wealth would be expropriated by the authorities, contrary to the way it is in some countries today, many of the best and most inventive entrepreneurial minds and talents became focused on wealth creation rather than simply wealth transfer.

In America, for the first time in human history, the expression "make money" became popular and accepted. People moved from all over the world, and still do today, for the opportunity to take part in the greatest entrepreneurial, wealth-creating system in all of human history.

Starting with Nothing

In fact, today, new immigrants to the United States are four times more likely to become millionaires than are native-born Americans who have lost sight of the key to becoming rich: Find a need and fill it.

Steve Siebold, author of the book *How Rich People Think*, said, "If you want to make a lot of money, find a big problem that a lot of people have, and solve it in a new way."

This is your key to wealth creation as well. And there is no other way to become truly wealthy except by supplying others with what they want and need and are willing to pay for.

Develop Rich Habits

In the simplest terms, rich people have rich habits, and poor people have poor habits. Mary Kay Ash, an amazing self-made millionaire, used to motivate her distributors by saying, "Don't get the rabbit habit; think mink."

Rich people think mink in every area of their lives.

I remember when I was in my thirties, still broke and struggling, working hard and making little progress, I enrolled in an executive MBA program at the local university. One evening, when I arrived for classes, a local well-known entrepreneur, wealthy and successful, pulled in to the parking space next to me driving a silver-gray 450 SEL Mercedes-Benz. I got out of my old Volvo and just stood there staring at his car. The driver looked at me, looked at my car, and then looked back at his car. He then smiled, waved, and walked off to class.

At that moment, I decided I was going to do whatever was necessary to become wealthy enough to be able to drive a big, beautiful, expensive Mercedes-Benz like that. I looked into the car and saw it had blue leather upholstery, and I made a mental note of that as I walked away.

Think Rich

From that moment onward, I began to think rich. I began to read two or three hours a day about the habits and behaviors of wealthy people. I got another job and then a better job. I took on more responsibility and moved up. I worked longer hours, sometimes twelve hours per day, and generated more and more money for my employer, some of which he paid out to me in the form of bonuses and profit sharing.

Within thirty-six months, I walked into the Mercedes-Benz dealership, traded in my car, laid my money down, and drove out in a silver-gray 450 SEL Mercedes-Benz with blue leather upholstery. It was one of the great moments of my life.

Develop the Habits

For you to develop rich thinking, to become wealthy, you must first develop the habits of thinking and of action that wealthy people have. Jim Rohn once said, "It is not becoming a millionaire that is important. It is the kind of person that you must become in order to become a millionaire that is even more important. Then, even if you lose all your money, you can earn it all back again because now you are the kind of person who knows how to make this kind of money."

Mike Todd, the film producer and husband of Elizabeth Taylor, once lost all his money on a big production and went broke. It was in the newspapers, and many of his "friends" laughed at him behind his back.

One of them asked him, "Mike, how does it feel to be poor?"

Mike Todd replied with these classic words. He said, "I've never been poor, only broke. Being poor is a frame of mind. Being broke is a temporary situation."

He then went back to work on his next project, which was successful, and in a couple of years he was rich again.

Nature Is Neutral

The Law of Cause and Effect, the great law of the universe, says that if you think and act like wealthy people, you soon become one of them. And if you don't, you won't.

Nature is neutral. Nature is like the statue of justice, with a blindfold. Nature plays no favorites. As Goethe said, "Nature understands no jesting; she is always true, always serious, always severe; she is always right, and the errors and faults are always those of man. The man incapable of appreciating her she despises; and only to the apt, the pure, and the true, does she resign herself, and reveal her secrets."

Fortunately, your mind is the one thing in the universe over which you have complete control, and that's all you need to get started.

Something-for-Something Thinking Versus Something-for-Nothing Thinking

This is a major difference in the thinking styles of rich people versus poor people. Rich people are always looking for ways to create value, to develop and produce products and services that enrich and enhance the lives and work of other people.

They are always willing to put in before they take out. They do not believe in easy money or something for nothing. Rich people believe that you have to justly earn and pay for, in terms of toil and treasure, any rewards and riches that you desire.

Poor people lack this fundamental understanding, the direct relationship between what you put in and what you get out. They are always seeking to get something for nothing or for as little as possible. They want success without achievement, riches without labor, money without effort, and fame without talent.

Poor people gamble, buy lottery tickets, come to work at the last possible moment, waste time while they are there, and then leave work at the first possible minute. They line up by the hundreds and thousands to audition for programs like *American Idol*, thinking that they can become rich and famous without ever having paid the price necessary to develop the level of talent and ability that enables them to rise above their competitors.

One of the great secrets of becoming wealthy is to always do more than you are paid for. If you do, you will always be paid more than you're getting today. And there is no other way.

Go the extra mile. Be willing to put in far more than you are taking out. There are never any traffic jams on the extra mile.

Developing New Habits

Fully 95 percent of everything you do is determined by your habits, first of thinking and then of action.

Successful people have good habits that lead to happy, productive, and financially successful lives. Poor people have poor habits, or no habits at all, that lead to the opposite. Fortunately, all habits are learnable with practice and repetition. You can learn any habit or skill you need to learn to achieve any goal you can set for yourself.

The only real question is, "How badly do you want it?"

Rich people and poor people have been studied, contrasted, and compared for many years to determine what it is about them that makes them different from each other.

The bottom line is that you can start off with every advantage in life—good family, excellent education, ideal contacts and opportunities—but if you lack the mental habits necessary for success, they will do you no good.

On the other hand, you can start with no advantages, like people who escape from a poor country or a dictatorship and arrive with no friends, no contacts, even no language skills, but with excellent habits, and then go on to create great lives for themselves.

The Seven-Step Strategy

Habits are developed with a simple seven-step strategy.

First, strive to develop only one habit at a time. If you get ambitious and decide to develop several good habits immediately, you end up developing none. Be patient. "Make haste slowly."

Because it takes about twenty to thirty days of repetition to develop a new habit, you can actually develop one new wealth-building habit per month, or twelve new habits in a year. This is enough.

For example, most wealthy people arise before 6:00 a.m., fully three hours before their first appointment. They have rituals that they follow each day. They get up, exercise, dress, plan, and prepare for the day.

They read, learn something, and get organized. They are

usually at work long before the average person has had his first cup of coffee. This is a habit you can decide to develop immediately. It may change your life.

Second, input new data: Decide upon a habit that can be helpful for you to develop. Be clear about this new way that you want to think and act. Turn this new habit over in your mind.

For example, rich people think about creating wealth most of the time. They look around continually for opportunities to make more money by offering products and services that people want and need, both today and in the future. They think continually about revenue generation. You can do the same.

Third, affirm to yourself that you already have this habit. Say to yourself, over and over, "I see money-making opportunities everywhere." The most powerful words are the ones you say to yourself and believe.

Continually read, learn, study, and gather information about making money. Read the interviews and stories of other people who have started with very little and become financially successful. Think about how you could do the same.

Fourth, visualize yourself as you would be practicing this new habit. Remember, "The person you see is the person you will be."

All improvement in your performance begins with a change in your mental pictures of yourself acting in a particular way. You always perform on the outside the way you see yourself performing on the inside.

Create a mental picture of yourself getting out of bed before 6:00 a.m. and immediately beginning your day. It is amazing how many wealthy people say that they start every morning, sometimes at 4:00 or 5:00, with thirty to sixty minutes of aerobic exercise. If you do this every day for a month, you will soon develop a positive addiction to the feeling of being bright, alert, and full of energy all day long.

Fifth, act as if you already had this new habit. There is a Law of Reversibility that you can use that is responsible for many of the great transformations in people that lead to financial success.

This law says that if you feel in a particular way, or if you believe yourself to be a particular type of person, you will naturally act in a particular way. But what if you start off not feeling or believing that you are a wealthy or successful person?

William James of Harvard pointed out, "If you do not already have a habit that you desire, act as if you already had this habit in every respect, and the action itself will soon create the actual belief."

Successful people plan every day in advance, usually the night before. They set priorities on their tasks and begin on the most important task first thing, before anything else. You can do the same thing, starting tomorrow.

As you plan and organize your day, think to yourself, "This is what rich people do." In no time at all, it will be a habit and will be locked in as a permanent part of your daily routine.

Sixth, refuse to allow exceptions. Once you resolve to develop a habit, never let up until the new habit is locked in permanently. Don't rationalize away unhelpful behavior. Refuse to justify or make excuses for not remaining true to what you have resolved to do. This is what poor people do.

Seventh, if you "fall off your horse," get back on immediately. If you lapse back into the old habit, which you will from time to time, immediately catch yourself and begin acting consistent with the new habit that you have decided to develop.

Brush off your temporary lapse and say, "Next time, I'll do better," and then begin again. Don't expect to get it right the first time, or even the first few times. Be patient and persistent.

Form Good Habits

Good habits are hard to form but easy to live with. Bad habits, on the other hand, are easy to form but hard to live with. The rule is for you to form good habits and make them your masters.

New habits are difficult to practice and learn at first, but soon they become automatic and easy. Soon it becomes easier to practice your new habit than to fall back into your old ways of doing things.

Habits of Wealthy People

You can develop several habits that are practiced by virtually all rich people. For example, in the *Forbes* 2015 survey of self-made billionaires, fully 76 percent attributed their success to "hard work and self-discipline."

Millionaires work about sixty hours per week, usually six days a week, ten or more hours per day. They arise early and get started by 7:00 or 8:00 a.m. and keep going until 6:00 or 7:00 p.m. As David Foster, the music impresario, said, "I don't know any successful people who work less than six days a week."

Do What You Love

Here's the key. Do what you love to do. Do work that you enjoy, that attracts you, energizes you, and makes you happy. Most millionaires say that they never work a day in their lives. They just do something they love to do and get paid very well for it. You should do the same.

In addition to working hard and having self-discipline, millionaires do not waste time. They think continually about revenue generation by serving their customers better, faster, and cheaper than their competitors, no matter what business they are in. They continually ask themselves, "Is this the most valuable use of my time in achieving my goals?"

Set Clear Goals

Most millionaires are intensely goal oriented. They have a major definite purpose, one big goal, sometimes called a BHAG (Big Hairy Audacious Goal) that they think about and work on all the time. What is yours?

Millionaires set measures, especially financial measures, and deadlines for each of their goals.

Millionaires are frugal, careful with their money. They examine every detail of an investment or an expense before making a decision. They like to earn money, but they hate to lose money.

Millionaires focus on financial accumulation, on earning and keeping more and more of their money. As the Japanese proverb says, "Making money is like digging in the sand with a pin. Losing money is like pouring water on the sand."

Use Your Time Well

Millionaires are highly productive and use their time well. They plan every day in advance. They set clear priorities on their time. They focus and concentrate on the most valuable use of their time every minute and every hour.

Poor people throw themselves at their work, without detailed planning, and end up wasting an enormous amount of time, becoming tired and discouraged long before they achieve success.

One of the most valuable skills you can learn is to calculate your desired hourly rate, or income. Divide the number 2,000, the average number of hours successful people work in a year, into your desired annual income. If your goal is to earn $100,000 per year, divided by 2,000 hours, this equals $50 per hour.

From then on, every minute and hour of every day, you ask yourself if what you are doing is paying you your desired hourly rate or more. If it isn't, you immediately stop doing it. You delegate, outsource, or eliminate that task. You absolutely refuse to do anything that does not pay you the kind of money that you have decided to earn.

Just Say No

As Nancy Reagan said, in advising teenagers about drug use, "Just say no!" Just say no to anything that is not the highest and best use of your time, to anything that does not pay you the kind of money that you want to earn.

When Warren Buffett was recently asked the secret of

his success, he replied immediately, "I just say no to everything."

John Doerr, the multibillionaire venture capitalist from Silicon Valley, has a complete staff whose job is to do everything except for the few things that only he can do that are responsible for generating tens of millions of dollars for the firm. He says no to everything else.

Keep Learning and Growing

Millionaires are always learning new ideas. They read, learn, and listen two to three hours a day. They subscribe to summaries of business books and articles, both written and audio. They know that one key idea, combined with their existing knowledge, can change the future of their business and maybe even earn them a fortune. They are convinced that the right idea exists somewhere, and they are constantly seeking it from every source possible.

Avoid the Television Trap

Rich people watch less than one hour of television per day. Poor people watch five to eight hours of television per day, only going to bed when they are too tired to watch, and then get up and turn the television on to start the day.

Television can be a wonderful slave but a terrible master. Your television can make you rich or make you poor. It will make you rich if you leave it off most of the time. It will make you poor if you sit and watch it hour after hour.

A recent study found that as people became wealthier and wealthier, they began to move their television set farther and farther from the center of family activity. The wealthiest people actually set up a "television room," a place where they have to get up, go down the hall, and get themselves seated to watch television in the first place. They make it as difficult as possible to watch television, including getting rid of their television sets completely.

Become Insatiably Curious

Another habit of wealthy people is that they ask a lot of questions and then listen closely to the answers. Middle managers and middle-income earners seem to talk a lot and pay little attention when others are speaking. Wealthy people ask a lot of questions, listen a lot, and even take notes, knowing that almost everyone can come up with valuable insights that can be useful in generating wealth and earning more money.

Maintain Your Health and Energy

Rich people take excellent care of their physical health. They keep themselves well-informed about the things they can do to live a longer, healthier, and better life.

It takes high levels of energy to be successful, to work long hours, to start earlier than others, and to work later. Rich people are continually seeking ways to increase their levels of energy.

One expert said that the most important asset of any business is rested executive thinking time. This is your most important mental asset as well. How can you get more of it?

Proper Weight

This is where proper weight is so important. Being overweight is associated with numerous health problems. One of them is that carrying extra pounds puts a strain on your body, burning up energy that you could be using for achieving the success you desire.

The five-word rule for weight loss is simply "Eat less and exercise more." Wealthy people eat nutritious foods and drink a lot of water. As a result, they have more energy, especially mental energy they can focus on getting more and better results and earning more money.

PROPER REST

According to Anders Ericsson, a psychologist at Florida State University, elite performers sleep an average of 8.46 hours each night. What he found was that peak performance is hard work. It takes a lot of energy. You simply cannot perform at your best for any period of time if you're only sleeping five, six, or seven hours per night. You need eight to nine hours of sleep to totally rest your body and recharge your brain for the day ahead.

PROPER EXERCISE

Wealthy people exercise an average of two hundred minutes per week, or about thirty minutes per day, or more. They get up and exercise each morning. They walk more often from place to place, take the stairs more often than the elevator, and are always looking for opportunities to move their bodies.

Someone once told me, "Every joint in the body is meant to be fully articulated every single day." That piece of advice has guided my personal exercise program for years.

Calculated Risk Taking

Rich people are willing to take risks to increase their wealth. But they do not gamble or take chances. They practice a special form of "risk avoidance" in the pursuit of higher income. They reduce risk that is inherent in anything new or different by gathering more and more information from every possible source.

Wealthy people are willing to move out of their comfort zones, to stretch themselves and try something new and different if that's what is necessary to achieve greater financial rewards. Rich people are continually seeking opportunities where they can apply their intelligence and resources to create wealth in new and different ways.

Rich people reduce investment risk by working with experts and by supervising their investments carefully. Once they have made the money, they are determined to hold on to it.

Network Continually

Rich people network continually. They are always looking for ways to broaden the number of their relationships with people whom they can help and who can help them. But as Baron de Rothschild once said, "Make no useless acquaintances."

Rich people do not spend their time with people who are going nowhere with their lives. They seek out the most successful people in their community and their industry and look for ways to spend more time with them. They stay away from negative people, those who criticize, condemn, and complain. If they find themselves with someone who is grumbling about life or work, they politely excuse themselves and go away.

Be a Joiner

Do what rich people do. Join one or two business associations that are important or helpful for your field. Attend the meetings. Identify the most important committees, and volunteer to sit on one of them.

The most important committees in any organization tend to attract the most important people within that industry. When you serve on these committees, you get an opportunity to meet and know these people in a neutral, nonthreatening environment. In a way, you get to "interview" with these people and let them see the kind of person you are by the quality of the contribution you make to your nonprofit organization.

The Most Important Quality

Perhaps the most significant quality of wealthy people is that they focus and concentrate on excellent performance, on getting better and better at the most important work they do.

In the final analysis, nothing will help you more in life than to develop a reputation as the "go-to guy or girl," the individual who is recognized as the very best performer in your particular area.

Just as the best investment that a company can make is in improving the quality of its product or service in terms of what its customers want and need, the very best investment that rich people make is in themselves, getting better and better in their key skill areas.

Your Future Is Unlimited

There have never been more opportunities for more people to earn more money and achieve their financial goals faster than exist today. But as Earl Nightingale said, "Before you can have something more and different, you must become someone more and different."

By the Law of Indirect Effort, when you focus single-mindedly on developing the thinking styles of wealthy people and engaging in the behaviors that they practice every day, you will soon become a wealthy person yourself, both on the inside and on the outside.

♦♦

ACTION EXERCISES

1. Resolve today to think and act like wealthy people. Practice the ideas in this chapter. Read the interviews, stories, and books about people who have become fabulously successful, and do the things they do.

2. Select one habit that you think can help you to develop the mind-set, the self-concept, of wealthy people, and work on that every day until it becomes automatic and easy for you.

3. Select one activity or lifestyle behavior of successful people and incorporate it into your lifestyle as well. Do it now.

SUMMARY

Success is not an accident. Failure is not an accident either. You are where you are and what you are because of yourself, because of your own thinking and behavior.

If you want your future to be better in any area, you must first change and improve your thinking along the lines described in this book. You must make new choices and better decisions.

Fortunately, everything you are today, you have learned from early childhood as the result of input and practice. At any time, you can decide to learn new ideas, practice new behaviors, and get different results.

Good luck!

ABOUT THE AUTHOR

Brian Tracy is chairman and CEO of Brian Tracy International, a company specializing in the training and development of individuals and organizations. He has studied, researched, written, and spoken for thirty years in the fields of economics, history, business, philosophy, and psychology and is the top-selling author of numerous books that have been translated into dozens of languages. You can contact him at briantracy@briantracy.com.